The Broken Notebooks

Also By John Gilmore

Head of a Man

Swinging in Paradise: The Story of Jazz in Montreal

Who's Who of Jazz in Montreal: Ragtime to 1970

JOHN GILMORE

The Broken Notebooks

Ellipse Editions

ELLIPSE EDITIONS

Copyright © John Gilmore 2018
All rights reserved

First Edition

No part of this work may be photocopied, reproduced, stored in a retrieval system, transmitted, or transported in any form by any means, electronic or mechanical, without the prior written consent of the author or publisher, or under terms agreed with the appropriate rights organization. Requests for copying any part of this book, by photocopying or other means, should be directed in writing to:

Access Copyright: The Canadian Copyright Licensing Agency
320 - 56 Wellesley Street West
Toronto, Ontario M5S 2S3 Canada
www.accesscopyright.com

For all other rights, contact the author or publisher

Cover photo (detail) © John Bigelow Taylor. Used with permission. Collection of The Museum of Cycladic Art, Athens, Greece

First published in Canada in 2018 by Ellipse Editions, an imprint of John Gilmore
ellipse.editions@mykolab.com

Set in Garamond, cover titles in Baskerville

Legal deposit: Library and Archives Canada, 2018

Gilmore, John, 1951 –

ISBN   978-0-9867866-2-4

Parts of this work were first published in Finland in the Swedish-language magazine *Presens*, translated by Heidi von Wright.

The creation of this work was made possible thanks to the financial support of the Conseil des arts et des lettres du Québec.

Participation in residencies supporting the creation of this work was made possible thanks to travel grants from the Canada Council for the Arts.

To my mother, Grace

*from what depths: from unspeaking
time – from a treasure forgotten?* [1]

– Gennady Aygi

I discovered that the subject I had chosen was immense and that selecting what sequences to include ... could only be arbitrary. That's why I invite the imagination of the reader or viewer to make liberal use of the elements that I put at their disposal. [2]

– Ingmar Bergman

Prologue

It's not easy to find the study room in the British Museum. We follow the directions given to us at the desk, but even then we have to ask again, of a guard in one of the galleries. He leads us to a door, and knocks for us. Someone leads us from there to an inner room and shows us the place where he will sit.

Observe: a clock is ticking, its mechanism resonant inside a wood cabinet on a wall. Observe: there are Roman numerals on its face. Notice, too, there are other people in the room, talking quietly, sparingly; work is being done, pages are being turned. Look up: the room is lit from a skylight high above. It's only then we notice the mezzanine encircling the room, a narrow catwalk leading past tall cabinets full of books and ledgers bound in leather, their spines impressed with gold lettering. Iron staircases ascend in tight spirals from the corners of the room.

There is a knock.

Someone goes to the door with a jangle of keys. Faces turn. He is greeted by the same woman who greeted us. After a brief discussion, he takes his place at the table.

And now we can begin.

He picks up an object from a tray that is placed in front of him. It is A23 in the Catalogue of Greek Sculpture in the British Museum.[3] *Parian marble, excavated by Bent.*[4] It is the body of a woman without clothing, her face flat and featureless except for the pronounced ridge of her nose. He turns her slowly in his left hand, exploring the ways she fits with his own anatomy. He perches her on his third finger and thinks to himself (feeling foolish at the thought) that she is like a pixie, a Tinker Bell, her arms folded impishly, leaning back against the fleshy pads of his fingers, feet dangling in mid-air. With his right hand he sketches her in his notebook, poorly, amateurishly, trying only for essentials. It will help him remember, more than the words he scribbles, estimates of size and weight, observations on colour, incrustation, calcification, terms he has learned from books.

> *Weight of an apple.*
> *Skin like marzipan.*
>
> *She grows warm in my hand – then gives warmth back.*

He, too, notices the clock ticking. *Comforting*, he writes. He hears voices, too, coming from the galleries. The words are unintelligible.

He picks up A23 again in his left hand. (He is conscious of the woman watching him, from behind her computer screen.) He lays her in the cup of his palm. Later he will write: *where we cup water and lift it from a stream*. For now he writes: *my first two fingers curl naturally around her shoulders*. As he writes he thinks, but does not write, *protectively*, and the thinking causes him to pause, remembering what an arm feels like around a shoulder.

> *Lie still.*
> *Lie still.*

Observe his face while he holds A23: calm immobility. A softening? The expression is imprecise. We cannot extract meaning from it, not with any hope of certainty. Better to continue observing, and hope clarity will come.

He is lingering now over another sketch. A23 is sitting on the fleshy pad at the base of his first finger. (He has no calluses.) His first finger is erect, but (– and he wonders if he ever noticed this before) his finger is not straight, it curves back slightly, as if bent back at the tip by some gentle, invisible hand. The act of drawing requires him to look closely. The back of the figurine marries perfectly the curve of his finger. The tip of her head ends precisely at the tip of his finger. He wonders if this holds meaning.

> *Lie still.*
> *Lie still.*

He turns A23 over and looks at her back. The sketch he makes this time is simple, almost schematic, for there is little anatomical detail on this side of her. (Later he learns that this is characteristic of the figurines, hence the descriptors *frontal* and *frontality*.) Her back is flat, from one side to the other. The curve that matched the curve of his finger is hardly visible, seen face-on. (When he strokes her back with his fingertip, then he feels it.) He draws a vertical line on the page. This is the line cut into the stone to represent her spine. The line stops before it meets another line, intersecting, not cut into the stone but protruding. This represents her buttocks. It is this *protuberance* (another word he learned from books) that sat on the pad at the base of his finger. Below her buttocks, the vertical *incised* line (another learnt word) continues downward, marking the separation of the thighs. At her knees, it changes: the incised line opens up into a narrow *cleft*. The stone has been cut open, all the way through to the other side, but only between the calves. It closes again at the ankles. Out of a sense of obligation (to what, he is not sure), he roughs in quickly the outer contours of her body, but it is the schema of those lines and that open space between her calves that he wonders about. Does this hold meaning?

Now observe: he lays A23 on the green felt that has been put on the table before him, on her back, as some believe she was meant to be, in imitation of the dead. He pushes back his chair and lays his cheek on the table beside her. He straightens up, self-conscious. This sketch, too, is quick and simple, but he goes over two lines again and again with his pen, darkening them, clarifying something he sees. The figurine is touching the table at only two points – the back of her head and the protuberance of her buttocks. His first darkened line, from head to buttock, is a single undeflected curve. (He wants to write "graceful, like an elongated arch under an old stone bridge," but he is afraid to appear foolish, undisciplined in his research.) His sketching continues, in quick light strokes: a small pyramid representing her breasts, a low rise for the round of her belly, and then her legs, elevated, her knees bent, her feet limp in midair (– *like babies we have played with*). But now observe the second line darkening under his pen: it is a straight line, as straight as he can make it freehand, from the protuberance of the buttocks to the back of the knee. Whether these lines are, in stone, as he emphasizes them on paper is not for us to judge. This is how he sees them and wants to remember them. He is writing now under his sketch, with arrows pointing to the body: *one long perfect sweep* and then *sharp point* (the buttocks) and then *straight line* (the back of the thighs). He wonders if this, too, might hold meaning. He is looking for a way in.

> *Contour subsumes meaning* (he writes later)
> *something releases, falls away*

Let us continue. He has put down A23 and taken up two other objects from the tray, one in each hand. These are A5 and A6. These, too, are called figurines, but they are barely representational of the human form. He has already learnt, from books, to call them *schematic* figurines. I might as well tell you, quickly, while he examines them: they are one more mystery. Some schematic figurines predate the more common representational ones, like A23, and can be thought of as precursors to them, trial runs, perhaps, at carving the human form. But other schematic figurines were carved concurrent with the most sophisticated representational figurines, so the decision to make one kind or the other was not determined by skill. By what, then? The catalogue says A5 and A6 were found in the same grave (Bent, again, 1884) and he knows from reading a book that Bent imagined them as male and female, as soul mates.[5] It is a romantic notion that has no place in any serious scholarship, but one he finds hard to put out of his mind.

He puts down A6, shifts A5 to his left hand. He draws two parallel lines, free-hand, in his notebook, one superimposed on one of the faint blue lines of the page, the other half-way to the next blue line. He writes: *thickness at the edge*. He draws two more parallel lines, superimposed this time on adjacent blue lines, and writes *thickness at the middle*. Then he sketches the figurine as it looks in his hand. The bumps that might be shoulders or the stumps of amputated arms fit easily in his hand, one in the saddle between thumb and first finger, the other in the V between his middle fingers. There are no legs: the flat bottom, at what might be hip level, rests on the fleshy pad at the bottom of his palm. The long neck, ending in a point, extends beyond his fingers.

> *stabbing*
> *thrust*
> *quick parry*
> *(a hunter)*

This is the male figurine of Bent's imagination, and it colours his own seeing. He is aware of that happening, but is intrigued nevertheless by the suggestiveness of the shape.

> *phallic neck*
> *broad shoulders*
> *straight flank*
>
> *lean*
> *powerful*
> *thrusting*

He sketches the female now, A6. She too has a long neck, but it does not end in a point; it ends bluntly. He draws again.

> *thicker*
> *doesn't lie flat*
> *notched waist*
> *rounded trunk*
> *feels chunky – flabby – pregnant?*

There is still one more figurine for him to examine, and time is running out. He has been allocated only these three hours. But let us pause and observe something that happens in the room, since he has paused to observe it, too. A telephone rings, for the first time all morning. The woman who greeted him converses quietly for a moment, then says goodbye. She reports to another person in the room that the caller is going to be late. "A huge traffic snarl-up," she says. "A possible terrorist alert." They go back to their work.

He picks up A17.

> *length of my arm*
> *too heavy to hold for long*

He needs two hands, one to support her neck, the other under her calves. He holds her this way, in front of his abdomen, elbows at his sides, and pauses. Then he puts her down.

> *walk forward with her into ceremony –*
> *she is built for ceremony –*
> *there is too much mass of her ever to warm to my touch*

Later he writes: *When I lay her on her back on the table and lowered my head to her side, she looked like a child's drawing of a bird: two long heavy wings arching out from the middle. But her buttocks were not resting on the table. Her whole body was suspended in air. It rested only at the ends, on the wing-tips of her head and her heels. It was a curious body, thick, without lightness or grace. Seen in profile like that, it was approximately the same thickness from wing-tip to wing-tip, as though the child had drawn with the thick edge of a marker pen: two strokes, two arches of stone.*

He stands up and looks down at her, lying on the table. *Her breasts were small mounds. One was higher on her chest than the other. Her* pubic triangle *was in relief, and blank – there was no incision for the vulva. Her legs were a single mass; there was no cut through, just a deep groove between them. Only her feet were separated, slightly splayed.* He sees a scar across her knees and asks the woman at the computer. Time is running out. She comes to the table and explains. The legs were broken; no one knows why. She arrived at the museum that way. A conservator rejoined them. The catalogue says she arrived in 1863, a gift of the heirs of a former British ambassador to Constantinople.[6] No one knows where she came from. *Provenance unknown,* is the term they use.

Provenance unknown.

The Broken Notebooks

Look down on the world, as a bird looks down: the islands are stepping stones across the sea we call the Aegean, from the land mass we call Asia to the land mass we call Europe. Humans have always crossed this way – migrants, traders, armies. The flyways of migratory birds pass over the islands, too: the birds stop and feed on their way to Africa, and, six months later, returning to northern Europe. Back and forth, rhythmically: swallows, yellow wagtails, warblers, wheatears. People of leisure come, too, from far away, on yachts and cruise ships, and ferries with names like Blue Star. Everything is in motion out here. Winds streak the world with spume. Waves turn up polished stone.

Sea beat our body.
Wind beat our body.
Sing of this –

It began at the moment of the book. It opened in his hand to a colour photograph of a 4,000-year-sculpture in stone.[7] The photographer had posed the figurine upright against a black backdrop and lit it from behind. It was a revelation, as if he were looking through the body of a woman. The figurine was translucent, glowing pale red where the stone had been carved thin. The rest, masses of darkness. *Red, like the webs between my fingers when I hold them up to a light.* Red that is unseen, until the moment of the wound.

Objectively, what did the photograph reveal to him? The frailness of stone. (– yes, even stone.) The crystalline nature of marble. The marks of stone tools. The text in the book told him this was a figurine of the Early Cycladic Culture, 3200 to 2000 BC, the form unchanged in pose and distinguishing characteristics for a thousand years, then never seen again – a ridge of nose on an otherwise featureless face, arms folded across the front, left arm above the right arm, feet together, toes pointing downward, the body unclothed.

> *What appears mass is less than mass.*
> *Light enters and leaves.*
> *(– as my love leaves no trace)*

The masses of darkness revealed in the photo: the density of throat and breast and pelvic cradle. He thought of song and milk and entry to the world. He could not say what the figurine offered. Only that the book opened to her.

We are waiting for him beside a stone wall. He will arrive soon by taxi, from the port town. Observe (as he soon will): There is no one about. There is no sound of human activity. After the taxi leaves, there will be no sound again except the wind, and the distant clanking of tin bells on the necks of grazing animals.

The wall is at the edge of a village. The village is very small, a hamlet. It doesn't appear to be anything more than a handful of white buildings, bunched together in one corner of a plateau. The plateau slopes downward gently towards the sea, and then appears to drop off abruptly.[8] Perhaps there are cliffs; we cannot see. The stone wall we are standing beside is a dry wall, without mortar, and in good repair. There is evidence that the field on the other side has been recently worked. But no one is about, in the fields or in the village or on the high hills that rise up behind the village, crossed with more stone walls. We are alone. There is only the wind blowing cold and hard out of the north. The sun is brilliant. Cumuli are hurtling overhead.

His taxi arrives down the winding road from the main road at the top of the ridge. It stops outside the village. He is paying the driver. He is asking something, with exaggerated gestures. The driver points into the distance, then his hand opens and sweeps across the windshield.

No one was about. Nowhere a marker. No sign.

He pulls a parka and a wool toque out of his pack and quickly puts them on. The taxi has dropped him at the juncture of three roads, beside a concrete pedestal at waist height. He surmises that it once held an interpretive panel, but the panel is gone, ripped from its fastenings. There is only a dark rectangular ghost on the broad, flat surface. Stone walls are everywhere and he cannot see where the roads lead. One seems to loop above the village. The other two drop below. The map he was given at the tourist office is no help. He isn't even sure where he is on the map, or whether the promontory at the edge of the sea is Kastri. The driver pointed in that direction, but it isn't the highest point of land. The ridge behind him is much higher, and a mountain looms over the village, to the north.

He does not enter. He does not want to intrude. (It's also true that he is wary of dogs.)

Observe: He is walking away from the houses, towards the other end of the plateau, along a narrow meandering road between high stone walls. On a gradient leaving the village, the road has been paved with concrete. Lines were scraped into the surface before it dried. He is struck by the pattern of the lines. He sketches it in his notebook, and recognizes it as the same pattern he has seen on bowls painted by the people who lived here 4,000 years ago.

The tourist map, deficient in detail and topography, has led him to believe that there is no direct path from the village to the summit of Kastri. In fact, there is. We are waiting for him at the trailhead. But he has chosen the road that leads towards open space. He wants what isn't there.

Chalandriani.
His arm swept open.

Chalandriani.
Just to say the name invokes something.
Just to voice it in the throat –
Chalandriani.

There where a great cemetery lay. Six hundred graves. Four thousand years.

Farmers found it, plowing, picking up stone. They kept figurines in their houses, as one keeps a sun-bleached antler on a window sill, or the feather of a hawk. I heard of an old woman who recalled playing dolls with a figurine when she was a little girl. Men of words heard the stories, too, and came to dig. The first systematic excavation was led by Christos Tsountas, 1898. He came with money, official papers, tools. Workers under his command opened the earth. He made notes, writing in pencil in a book-keeper's ledger, writing to the edge of the page, ignoring the faint red lines meant to order columns of figures. His script was small, cramped, like the graves he looked down into. He drew floor plans, sketching diagrams of the graves in his notebooks, number 333, number 334, triangulating shapes, recording the length of sides and the distances corner to corner. 8 mm. 107 mm. 96 mm. 15 mm. Every angle could be calculated, every grave reconstructed. The notebooks are in a museum, lying under glass. I heard of a man who calculated every melodic interval in a solo by John Coltrane, tabulated their frequency of occurrence, how many times the line leapt a sixth, fell a whole tone, bent a quarter. He was convinced something of importance would be revealed that way.

Tsountas excavated cemeteries on other islands, too, and was the first to recognize a distinct culture on the Cycladic islands during the period of human development we call the Early Bronze Age, four thousand years ago. It was a prehistoric age, meaning writing had not yet been invented. There are no written records, no manuscripts or parchments, no words chiseled into stone that might explain why the Early Cycladic Culture thrived for more than a thousand years, then mysteriously disappeared.

Tsountas's pioneering work sparked more excavations in the early years of the 20th century. Then the Second World War intervened, followed by the Greek Civil War, and it wasn't until 1949 that archaeological research resumed. But interest in Early Cycladic Culture remained marginal until the 1950s and early 1960s, when Picasso, Modigliani, Brancusi, and other artists praised the

Cycladic figurines, and their influence became apparent in modern art. Suddenly, objects once dismissed as ugly, "primitive" curiosities became the talk of the art world, sought-after commodities on the international art and antiquities markets. The result was a rush of forgeries and, worse, a frenzy of looting. Early Cycladic cemeteries were plundered and destroyed as figurines and other grave goods were smuggled out of Greece to fill museums and private collections around the world. Archaeologists were unable to keep pace with the looting, and soon found themselves excavating cemeteries that had already been plundered. It was not all nightmare: the 1960s also saw a profusion of publications, the development of scientific procedures to test the authenticity of artifacts, and efforts to try to stop the smugglers. But it was mostly too late. Looting, driven by the demands of the market, had effectively destroyed the archaeological record.[9]

He is looking out over empty spaces. He can see other islands and the straits between them, and wind-driven swells, white-flecked. He cannot see deeper motions, but he imagines them: *hidden currents, eternal forces*. The wind sweeps down hard from over the bare ridge, pummelling him with a force that surprises him, knocking him off balance. The light is brilliant, cleansing, charged with racing shadows. He relishes the silence between gusts: he imagines there is nothing there.

What happens on the plateau is hard to define. No one thing of any consequence happens. He follows the road. He walks into the distance. He follows where the roads leads, between stone walls so high they sometimes block the view. When the undulation of land and road allow him a glimpse over the wall, he sees an emptiness he has never experienced before.

He wants it to be simple: an abstract intersection of planes. He wants to strip everything to its essence: a sloping plane of land, a plane of sea, a plane of tilting sky. He wants to see all this without adornment, as the figurines are without adornment. As the land was, four thousand years before.

The plateau corresponds to something in him that he cannot articulate. It is perhaps the place from which he will never leave. There is space to walk out into, and perhaps that is why, though his purpose here is anything but aimless, he seems in no hurry to turn and walk towards Kastri. But perhaps that is only surface we are seeing. He has given himself this task, to understand, a task which relieves him of the anxiety that he is doing nothing of value. Visiting Kastri gives him purpose, however artificial, a reason to explain his presence here, at this late time of year, after the tourists have gone home. But that is still surface: underneath, he is drifting.

He passes a brown sign on a post, pointing onward to Kastri. He finds that strange, because he is sure now that the promontory behind him is Kastri. He looks again at the tourist map and thinks perhaps the trailhead is still ahead, the dotted line that will lead down towards the sea and the ascent route up Kastri. A few minutes later he comes to another juncture of roads and another post and the same brown sign pointing onward. But below it, on the same post, is another sign to Kastri, this one blue. It points back from where he has come.

Shadows race out to sea. The wind is so strong he has to stoop and write notes in the lee of his own body, then push the notebook into the pocket of his parka before turning back into the wind. He writes, *crumbling edge of the continent*. We are losing him to imagination.

Chalandriani. People were born and died and buried here. A battle was fought here, possibly several, with spears and clubs and bare hands. Trees were cut down, boats built, metals forged. Grains were planted, winnowed, and ground to flour. Skins were scraped and cured and cut to fit the human form. Graves were dug, and walled, and tended, stone schist carried here to roof the bodies in.

In the museum, circumstances dictated focus, cultivated an expectation of result. There he could believe in the possibility of answers, though he had been forewarned by books that there were mysteries that might never be solved. The study room inspired faith in method and reason. Here, on the plateau, everything moves counter to method. The land is criss-crossed with walls. He chides himself for not being methodical, in earnest pursuit of the summit. But something in him wants to defy the straight line, the shortest distance.

Four songbirds in a tumble – five?

He is moving through imagined space, a space made of words he has read in books.

He observes the walls. Some are taller than he is: new stones laid on old stones: some are three metres high. Flat stones. Slabs an inch thick, or two inches thick, stacked dry, the bottom layers clotted with soil and plant growth, higher layers stained orange and white with lichen. The topmost slabs are clean. *Where*, he writes, *did the lower slabs come from? Were they taken from the opened graves?*

The cemetery is the most extensive Early Cycladic burial ground known. More than 600 graves have been excavated. The cemetery comprises two sections, a Western and an Eastern, in both of which the graves are arranged in clusters.[10]

I came to an opening below a stone wall. Without a flashlight I couldn't see the bottom; it ended in darkness. The mouth was blocked with a wood pallet, wired in place. I could see human things inside – pieces of twine, a tin mug, a roll of plastic sheeting, a clump of kindling.

I wanted bones.

Later, I realized: a shepherd's cave, a shelter.

As if a grave were anything more.

I wanted evidence. Some mark of the land remembering. Chalandriani. Human settlement. 3rd millennium BC. Generations of families. Generations of dead. I had seen drawings of the way they buried their dead. I had seen photographs in the local museum, the Tsountas excavation, a skeleton lying curled in fetal position, its possessions in front of it, hands raised to its lips. Chalandriani, human settlement, 3rd millennium BC. I wanted graves.

The graves are subterranean of polygonal or rounded plan, or a mixture of both. Their walls are constructed of flat stones in overlapping courses, without mortar, forming a false dome, the aperture at the centre of which is covered by a large capstone. The entrance frequently has a threshold and jambs of upright slabs, and is blocked by a slab or dry-stone walling.... The corpse was inhumed in contracted pose and not covered with earth. The head often rested on a stone slab acting as a pillow.[11]

Once this was forest, leaf underfoot, animals hiding. Generations of trees, dying, toppling, uprooted by storms. Layers of humus, worm-rich and moist. I wanted graves, and the very land itself was one. The hills above me were bare, denuded, deforested, their topsoil washed into the sea. The plateau of Chalandriani still bore earth, there were vegetable plots and pastures of sparse grass and wild thyme. But mostly it was stone: walls of stone, new stone heaped upon old stone. And still, the fields were covered with stone.

What draws him on are graves, the idea of them. He is not ready for the climb up Kastri. He sees clearly now that he is walking away from it, that this is not the way to a trailhead. But he goes on. There is nothing out there, he can see that, when the walls allow him to see. Only more walls, demarcating more fields. But he goes on. He needs to absorb something underfoot.

I forgot about time
the silting in and the plowing over –

For a whole afternoon I walked and found nothing.

We go with you. Always with you.

It was only later that it dawned on me. I had been walking on graves. The road, the village, the walls – all built over the graves of the dead. Where did Tsountas take the bones? Or did he cover them over, bury them again, this time for good?

What they found:

marble figurines
a stone pestle
bronze axes and fishhooks
obsidian blades
clay molds for casting metal
bronze awls and needles, pins and tweezers
a hollow bone stuffed with blue pigment
red and blue pigment, in bowls
clay bowls
marble bowls
a clay vessel in the shape of a frying pan[12]

The land is woman, swollen with gift.

Every inch of the earth, sacred to the memory. Thousands of years of our species walking upright on the earth, dying on the earth, buried in the earth, sacred ground. What is the time limit, the statute of limitations, on the sanctity of graves? When can they be plowed over, planted, paved, or built upon? When the bones have turned to dust? When all memory of the dead is gone? We move stele, grave stones, whole tombs into museums – but what of the graves marked only with a song?

We go with you. Always with you.

I clambered down through terrace after terrace, fig and pomegranate, until the terraces ended and there was only a wall and no way to go on. The wall was made of stones topped with a jumble of rebar and old wood shutters jammed together. This was not the way. I was below the highest point of the promontory, inland of it, at the edge of a raw drop. What lay below was hidden by a tangle of willow and bamboo clattering in the wind. When the rains came, it would be a torrent down there, water running fast off the denuded hills, flushing the creek bed out to sea. Rain or dry, it was impassable. I worked my way back up, conscious of trespassing. A dog barked above me, but no one appeared. The sheep and goats were waiting for me at the top. One goat was hobbled, her front legs tied together, her udder full. It was then, I think (– and this is how stories are born) – it was then I looked down and saw the arrow on the stone, the red paint scuffed and faded, pointing in the opposite direction. I looked ahead and saw another faded arrow, on another stone in the path. They were leading away from the gully and the promontory, in a wide arc around a walled field – and onward towards the sea.

Kastri, the approach.

He wants this to be harder than it is, to have the satisfaction of a better tale. Truth, it is not hard at all, once you get your bearings and set your mind to it. In summer, tourists do it in sandals, in the heat of day, for the view and the exercise, then drop back down to the beach and walk naked into the sea. But this is winter, and he is alone, and there is no one to be seen anywhere, and he is conscious of how a twisted ankle up there could suddenly turn life-threatening, exposed to the cold and wind through a long November night.

Slept fitfully. My body is tired this morning, and I'm vaguely despondent. Perhaps it's the recognition that I have so little to go back to, after the phone call last night. I think of taking a bus to another part of the island, to sight-see, but I'm tired and wanting refuge in my room. I buy some food at the market, come back, make tea in a small cup with water from a kettle that never boils.

He is in the museum, struggling to make himself understood.
He points to the enlargement of an old photograph on the wall: an open grave, a skeleton, intact, lying on its side.
– Where? he asks, pointing from the photograph to a map on another wall.
Everywhere, her hand circles.
– Bones? he points again, and gestures to his eye. – See? Where?
Taken, she tugs at the air.
She smooths the air flat in front of her, everything is covered now.
She bleats like a sheep, giggles, shrugs, and walks away.

We go with you. Always with you.
Do not be afraid.

They gave me a booklet. The map was useless. It was the photographs that persuaded me to try again. That *was* Kastri – I was looking right at it – that *was* the path, the red arrows on the stones. The next day I walked straight to it, no diversion, no backtracking. The sheep and goats seemed to be waiting for me, and when I set off along the red arrow path, they clanked and bumped after me on the other side of the wall.

      lizards scurry under rocks
      water bottles, beer cans
      a Marlboro pack

      a box
      emptied of 12-gauge shells

            Rottweil
            Loaded in Greece

the wind drives streams of foam across the sea
flings my hat to the ground

    in lulls —
               songbirds

    in lulls —
                            rise
            bees
                                drift to another blossom

A geologist could explain why this upthrust withstood erosion, its inland face parting the torrents that have swept down off the hills over millennia, cutting ravines on both sides. Kastri is a natural fortress, a rock that resisted. If parties had landed on the other side of the island and approached over the ridge, the settlement on the plateau would have been vulnerable. But the promontory could have easily been defended in an age when killing was at the end of a spear.

Parties could have landed on the beach beside Kastri, and climbed the slope that I climbed. Or scaled the cliff at the toe of the rock. Either way, the attack would have been uphill, the attackers exposed to a rain of stones and spears, the defenders always on higher ground and, if necessary, withdrawing strategically in stages, to higher ground again. Only superior numbers could have defeated them, and or a long starvation siege. The fortress walls themselves were designed to channel attackers into entrances no wider than a spear thrust. First an outer wall, with only one opening, blind to what lay inside. Then open ground to an inner wall, where fighters waited inside bastions made of stacked stone, the walls so thick an attacker could only get at the defender by climbing up the outside of the bastion itself, exposing his belly to a spear thrust from below.

But to live up here? Where the water source? Where the shelter from driving winter rains?

The settlement [on Kastri] has a pericentric plan with most of the buildings arranged in insulae spreading towards the summit. The insulae are separated by steep and often stepped lanes.... The buildings themselves are one- or two-roomed, of trapezoidal or rectangular plan, and usually have rounded corners. The two rooms are invariably at an angle to each other and are rarely aligned on the same axis. The masonry is the same as that of the fortification but the main building material is small thin slabs of marble.[13]

Chalandriani, the largest cemetery ever found, generations succeeding generations on the fertile plateau. And then, the culture's collective energy turned to war, defence, preparation for battle. Fortifications were built. At the same time, fewer figurines were made, they were less refined, they deviated more and more from the canonical form the people had made for a thousand years. Something passed away. Hints of influence appear in other cultures – Crete, Turkey, mainland Greece – but it's all speculation. What happened? A geological cataclysm? A volcanic eruption? Invaders from Asia? Refugees displacing them from islands further north? What threatened them so deeply? All we know is that 1,200 years after it began, Early Cycladic culture ended. No more figurines were made, Chalandriani and Kastri were abandoned, and henceforth the region was dominated by another culture, the Minoan, based on the island of Crete.

All traces gone. Only speculation remains – speculation piled upon speculation, stone upon stone.

He hears a woman's voice, but no one appears. He thinks other people are climbing up after him, but no one appears. All day on top, he thinks of that voice, clear in the wind.

The white stone spoke.

Transcript: Yannis Maniatis, archaeometrist.[14]

I'm a scientist, not an archaeologist. But I've been working in archaeology for more than 25 years. I'm an archaeological scientist, an archaeometrist, as we call the discipline now.

What is marble, exactly?

Marble is made of calcium carbonate. $CaCO_3$. It's the same chemical formula as chalk and limestone. The difference is that marble has been metamorphosed, it's been heated under pressure in the earth, which makes it hard and crystalline.

Where did the Early Bronze Age people get the marble to make the figurines? Did they quarry it?

They didn't have to. They took it from outcroppings, and in this part of the world, the marble in the outcroppings fragments horizontally, in slabs. It doesn't break off in large blocks. That's why the figurines are flat. The people levered the marble off the outcroppings, or picked up pieces that had fallen on the ground. In our lab, we can analyze the crystal structure of a figurine and compare it with a database of marble samples we've collected from veins and quarries all over Greece and the eastern Mediterranean. So we can prove that many of the figurines found on Keros were made from marble from Naxos. But not from the famous quarries on Naxos – those were dug much later. The marble from the quarries is coarse-grained. The figurines were carved in fine-grained marble, and that comes from surface outcroppings.

I've read that the figurines were originally painted. Almost all the pigments have washed away, leaving bare marble again. But what were those pigments? How were they made?

The most common colours were red and blue. Red was usually made from cinnabar, or mercury sulphide: HgS. It's a natural mineral found in rocks. It's bright red or orange-red. The Early Bronze Age people probably took it from veins found at the surface. They made a pigment from it by grinding the cinnabar to a powder, then adding water and some kind of organic binding agent, maybe a plant resin. It's so long ago that the organic material has decomposed completely, so we'll never know what the organic glue was that made it stick to the marble. There are also some rare cases where we've found the red pigment was made from hematite, or iron oxide: Fe_2O_3. This produced a more earthy colour, a darker red. The word hematite comes from the Greek haima, meaning blood.

What about the blue?

That comes from azurite, a kind of copper carbonate. The formula is $2CuCO_3.Cu(OH)_2$. It's a natural mineral, too, found in rocks. Some traces of black pigment have also been found on a few figurines, but this is rare. The black is carbon black, like charcoal, made from charred wood or charred bone. There is no formula; it's almost pure carbon, pure C.

Did they use berries or plants to make pigments?

I don't think so. And remember: painting marble was common throughout Greek history. It wasn't just the Early Bronze Age people that did it. The ancient Greeks painted their marble, too, after they carved it. Everything was painted, sculptures, buildings – even the Parthenon.

I've seen these terms in books – *patina, incrustation, erosion* – but I'm not sure I understand exactly what they mean. How are they different?

Patina is staining on the surface of the stone. The stain may penetrate a little way into the stone, but not to its core. The principle cause is iron oxide in the soil, which produces a reddish or brownish patina. *All soil has some iron oxide in it, but depending on where the figurine was buried, the amount and colour of the patina will be different. A second cause of patina – but only in some figurines – is an impurity in the marble itself. The impurity is a mineral called pyrite. When it's exposed to the air, pyrite oxidizes and stains the marble red. Some of the marble from Naxos has pyrites in it, but not the marble from Paros.*

And incrustation?

Incrustation means that minerals have been deposited on the surface of the marble. They stick to the surface. The minerals come from the soil or nearby rocks. The binder material that attaches the minerals to the marble is calcium carbonate, the same material that marble itself is made from. One way incrustation happens is when water drips from a rock onto a figurine: incrustation slowly builds up on the surface of the figurine. It's similar to the way stalagmites build up on the floor of a cave.

Was it water dripping onto a figurine that caused the erosion, too?

No. The erosion on the figurines is not mechanical erosion. It's chemical erosion caused by acidity in the immediate environment of the figurine. The acid attacks the surface of the marble, dissolving the calcium carbonate around the grains of the stone. The rough surface we see is the grains themselves sticking out. Erosion can go as deep as 2 mm on some figurines.

Where does the acid come from?

From plants and acidic rocks. These can vary greatly, even within a small area, so the amount of erosion from one figurine to the next can vary greatly, too, even in the same cemetery.

What about the human body in the grave? The figurines were lying beside a decomposing body. Did the chemicals in the body have any effect on the figurine?

No. Decomposition is a fast process. The body is gone in a few years. The figurines have been lying in the ground for thousands of years.

But bones last a long time. Don't they have calcium in them?

Yes, but it's a different kind of calcium than the calcium found in marble. The bones didn't contribute to the incrustation on the figurines.

I notice you have a couple of reproductions of Cycladic figurines on your window sill. How do you look at them? Do you see them aesthetically or scientifically?

[laughs] *No one has ever asked me that before!* [pause] *I'm a scientist, an archaeometrist. People give me objects to analyze. When I get a figurine in my hands, it's not aesthetic, it's just an object. It's a subject of research. I see it first as a scientific problem to solve. But after, after I've finished analyzing it, if I put it on my desk and stand back and look at it, then I see it differently – as something man-made, amazing, and beautiful.*

A woman will have to enter the story somewhere. He cannot be alone forever. Although, he might say, he has his woman: the figurine from grave 28. He carries with him a picture of her, a photocopy from a book. He chose her, let us say, for practical reasons. Time was passing, it was expensive to stay in the capital, and his purpose was not to spend forever in libraries and museums, but to walk on the land. He wanted a structure for his wandering, a reason for making a particular island a destination. He was already thinking of the book he would write. He wanted an armature to hang a story on, a beginning and an end, a through-line around which everything else would coalesce. He imagined (while he was still in the library, surrounded by books) a cemetery on an island, the graves visible and cordoned off, and a site plan on an interpretive panel. And he would have with him a map, copied from the record of the excavation, and he would find grave 28 and perform a silent ritual standing in front of it, perhaps only imagine the ritual out of fear of looking foolish if someone else was there, too. In that way, he would complete his journey, and complete her journey, the figurine's, back to the piece of ground she was buried in, her resting place. Of course, she would always remain behind glass in the museum in the capital, but he would have her picture with him, and he would take out her picture when he found her grave, and something would become clear to him then. And he would feel he had brought her home, and then he himself could go home. Bringing her home – a spine for his story, a purpose for his journey, the stuff of a good book.

When I set myself that purpose, I still hadn't been to the islands, had never seen an archaeological site, had no sense of the land and the scale of things. I imagined a cemetery as we know it today. I imagined the military cemeteries I had seen in photos, the graves numbered even when the names of the dead are unknown. I hadn't yet grasped the enormity of the mystery, the looted graves, the archaeological sites destroyed by raw human greed. I hadn't thought what that would mean, until I began looking at figurines in the museums in Athens, looking for the one I would adopt as my own. It was then I began to sense the scale of the destruction – figurine after figurine unprovenanced. Some were attributed to an island, some even to a known cemetery, but nothing more. The National Archaeological Museum displayed only provenanced figurines from authorized excavations, but had no published catalogue of the figurines in their collection. The Museum of Cycladic Art had a catalogue, but in vitrine after vitrine the labels read: *provenance unknown, provenance unknown*. I made notes in the national museum, of the few figurines that had a grave number attached, and consulted books in the library of the British School at Athens. After a week of searching and cross-checking, I found her.

She was not particularly striking, or beautiful. She was not large. I could have picked her up easily with one hand. Her face and upper arms were deeply pitted with erosion, her back was incrusted with minerals that had dripped onto her in the grave. There was the barely discernible outline of an eye and mouth, where the stone had been protected from erosion by paint that had long ago washed away. (Archaeologists call these *paint ghosts* – they are rare.) All of this gave her a wizened look, like that of an old woman – youthful beauty gone, face wrinkled, body scarred. Four thousand years ago she had been buried in a cemetery called Phyrroges, somewhere in the southwest corner of Naxos. At the beginning of the 20th century she had been dug up by an archaeologist named Stephanos and her grave assigned the number 28 in the records of the excavation. Now she stands in a glass case in the National Museum of Archaeology. She does not command attention amidst the other objects. She is poorly lit. She stands on a small Plexiglass cube, anchored to a back support by a thin plastic thread around her neck. Beside her is the clay jug that was entombed with her. The National Archaeological Museum has labelled her number 6140.19. I found a photograph of her in a book, made a photocopy, and folded it inside a Ziplock bag.[15]

> We are joined, this one and I
> two undistinguished bodies
> torn from our land —

Transcript: Olga Philaniotou, archaeologist.[16]

What is the missing piece of information that would solve the mystery of the figurines? What do you hope to find one day that will tell you what they mean?

We will never know. There was no written language, so there is no hope of finding an inscription in stone that would explain them. Later periods had writing; that's how we know what sculptures meant, who they represented, the names of gods, and the stories about them.

But what if you find a shrine or temple from the Early Bronze Age?

How would we know it's a shrine or temple? Look at all the little churches all over Greece. They are sacred sites, but they are tiny. If one of the churches collapsed and an archaeologist excavated it a thousand years from now, there would be no way to distinguish it from a shepherd's hut — it's just a pile of stones.

So there will never be anything more than speculation about the meaning of the Cycladic figurines?

I'm not comfortable with certainty about a period for which I have no written sources. There is a lot of speculation. If you find obsidian on Keros, you can scientifically prove that it came from Melos. That's a fact. You can prove it. But who brought it there — that's where speculation begins. And you will never have an answer. People who have theories are certain they are right — but it's all speculation. We'll never know.

What do *you* think they mean? How do you read the figurines?

They tell us things about the people who made them — they had a good sense of proportion, they had a clear mind. They tell us that the people of the Early Bronze Age had a certain attitude to life — a very positive attitude — because of the peacefulness of the figurines. They're not monstrous, or ugly; they don't convey fear. But it's difficult not to project our modern mind onto them. It's impossible to be objective.

There are eight sculptures on stands waist high. At first glance they look like large bowls. But each is different; they are sensual shapes, waves of marble lapping back on themselves, rivulets of marble turning inside out like an Escher print. All could hold liquid, but they are abstractions, fantasies, as if the marble itself were flowing. I try to say this to him, knowing his English is limited, and I speak no Greek. I say the word *fluid* and his eyes light up. "Yes! Marble comes to us from the sea."

He leads the way into the garden, along a marble path. The patio table is polished marble. The patio deck is marble. The window sills of his house are marble. He goes inside to prepare tea.

Petros Dellatolas: born on Syros, his mother's island, raised on Tinos, his father's island. Raised in a village on a mountainside. His father was a marble worker; so were his uncle and cousins. Petros started chipping at marble when he was five. "I am a marble worker. Fifty years." He has worked in quarries, in cemeteries and museums. He has helped restore churches and archaeological sites. He is helping now to build exhibits for a museum on Tinos about the history and traditions of marble-working.[17]

There are two Tinoses, he explains: on the east side, farming has been the mainstay. On the mountainous west side, the land is not as good. "The people lived with stone." By which he also means, they lived *by* stone. More than half the population on that end of the island still makes a living from marble, in one way or another. Young men and women come from all over Greece to study marble-working at The School of Fine Arts in the mountain village of Pirgos. Petros studied there when he was a boy.

I pull out my photocopy of the figurine from grave 28. I say this is why I have come to the islands. I tell him I've been to museums, handled the figurines, talked to archaeologists. I tell him I've been to Syros, have visited Chalandriani and Kastri. I tell him I want to understand the figurines, how they were made and what they mean. I say the word *mystery* – and he interrupts. "It is *not* a mystery. These people made symbols. This was before writing. These were basic symbols." He struggles for a way to explain. "You see the church?" (I told him I had been to the Church of Panagia Evangelistria that morning, a famous site of Christian Orthodox pilgrimage on a hill overlooking the port town.) "You see the lamps?" Hanging from the ceiling in the chapel are lamps. "Under each lamp, there is something – yes? – a boat, or an arm, or food. These are symbols that everyone knows. It's not art. It is like road signs: no words, just symbol." He points to the picture again. "These were symbols. But we don't know what they mean."

He leads the way to his studio next door. It's a large, high-ceilinged building made of cinderblock walls, with large doors at one end and a covered terrace outside where two sculptors are working under his guidance. He picks up a slab of marble. He shows me the veins running parallel in the flat surface of the stone: this, he explains, is the "face" of the marble. The ends of the slab that cross the veins at right angles are the two "heads" of the marble. The edges of the slab running parallel to the veins he calls the "*morello.*" Each part of the marble – the face, the head, and the *morello* – must be worked differently, he says.

I stop him and tell him I want to be sure I understand. Is the Cycladic figurine as we look at it, face on – is that also the "face" of the marble? Yes, he says, there are two "faces" to the raw stone; they become the front and back of the figurine. And the two "heads" of the stone become the top and bottom of the figurine? Yes. And the sides of the figurine, is that the *morello* of the stone? Yes again. And the figurines were flat because the veins of marble that come to the surface on these islands fracture horizontally, in flat slabs? He says yes again and shows me again the veins in the stone. You must use different techniques for each part of the marble, he stresses. The "face" of the stone is the easiest to work. Chipping or grinding away at the *morello* is possible, but difficult. Cutting across the grain at the "head" is hardest of all.

Petros is certain that the people who made the figurines worked on the ground. How do you know? I ask. Because that's the way people worked on marble as recently as when he was a boy. They made a box out of four slabs of marble, one-or-two feet high, and filled the box with pebbles or sand or what he calls "sand of the marble" – the dust and fine particles left over from grinding and shaving. Then they hollowed out an impression in the sand and lay the piece they were working on in the hollow. The sand held the work in position and absorbed the shock of the chisel and hammer; otherwise, the marble would shatter if struck while lying on another stone. Even now, he says, if he's working on a small piece, he will lay it on a sack filled with marble dust, either on the floor or on a work table. He drops to the floor quickly to demonstrate the old working position, one knee touching the ground, the other up, like a sprinter "ready" in the starting block. He says he's sure the Early Bronze Age carvers worked the same way, on the ground, except perhaps when they were working on very small figurines, or when they were finishing pieces; then, he says, they probably lay an animal skin on their lap and worked there.

I ask if he prefers power tools or hand tools. He shows me a power grinder and says it's a hand tool, too. The grinder wheel is carbide. Another grinder has a diamond wheel. He picks up a steel hammer and chisel, gripping them firmly in his massive hands, and taps one against the other. Then he picks up a compressor hose and puts the chisel in a socket in the end of hose, and tells me this will do the same as the hammer, only faster. He says sometimes he works faster with hand tools than with power tools, and he prefers doing the initial roughing out of ideas with hand tools, because the pace of hand work gives him time to think and create. "We work together," he says – he and the marble.

The next day.

An old Corolla hatchback, a working car: dust, rattles, and pings. We race up the coast road, Petros reading the land for me while he drives. "There! And there! See?" He is pointing out marble veins coming to the surface. He traces a vein visible as a white line far below us, on our left, near the sea, then points to where the same vein emerges from the land beside the road, on our right. Marble, everywhere. An island of it. "Here is marble," he says. "You take a piece, and you work."

We are climbing on twisting roads, clouds racing low overhead. Some clouds are below us. We pass his home village, Kardiani. He slows and shows me an exposed marble face cut into the hillside above the road. "I worked there." He points to a bowl cut into the face: "My father made that." He waves his arms: there are quarries all around here that his family worked. I ask if the quarries are still being worked, or if he himself still takes marble from here. No, he says, it's too hard to get the marble out; there are no draft animals and their handlers anymore to drag the stone out to the road.

We drive on up into the mountains. He is pointing out more veins of marble, pointing to marble boulders lying on the ground. He points to a house where a marble worker lives – that one cuts stone for streets and gardens. He explains that most marble workers just cut stone; only a few work as artists. But some villages up here have three or four marble artists, and many of them have studios in Athens.

"This mountain is marble."

We race on.

We pull in for a look at a "marble factory." A man directs an overhead crane with a control box dangling from a cable. Another man grinds a slab of marble with a power tool. Petros says marble from three quarries on the island is brought here to be cut and trucked away.

Next stop: the blacksmith. His small workshop is right next to the road. The stone walls are half-a-metre thick. The roof is made of marble slabs lying on rough-hewn wooden rafters supported by a steel I-beam running the length of the roof. An anvil sits on an old tree stump near the forge. The blacksmith, a younger man with a beard and ponytail, swings a plastic pail up off the floor and onto a table. It's full of steel chisels that he makes for the marble workers of Tinos. Petros chooses six, examines the tips carefully, then the blacksmith wraps them in old newspaper and the transaction is done.

We drive only a few hundred metres further and stop. Petros is taking me to an abandoned quarry. We head up a steep footpath at a fast pace: I'm breathing hard and struggling to keep up. We come to the lip of the quarry, and walk down into a landscape of stone – stone walls, stone huts, stone pits, and exposed faces. The red soil is sprinkled with marble chips. Petros points out a stone shelter where the workers kept their tools. Sometimes they worked on small marble pieces in there, too, when it rained. There are several other shelters in the quarry, all made of stone, some half buried in the ground, like bunkers. I peer into one and find two graveyard crosses leaning against a wall. Petros says the quarry workers roughed out the crosses here, then sold them to a carver in town for finishing; these ones were abandoned. There are several pits, several exposed faces and veins, and piles of marble all around. Petros says there is still good marble here, but the quarry is not accessible by road, so it was abandoned sometime after the war. "Its all economy now – with machines." This quarry was worked by hand, tool makers working side by side with marble workers. Petros explains: Marble blocks were broken out of a vein by cutting a line of small holes at the depth required for the block. Then steel wedges were driven in slowly along the line of holes until the block lifted and fractured – because, he reminds me, the marble here fractures horizontally. Once the block was broken free of the vein, the men used steel bars to manoeuvre it onto a wood sled. Then a bull or cow dragged the sled uphill out of the pit, while the men levered it from behind with their steel bars. At the top of the incline, the sled was dragged down the path to the road.

We head back up the incline. At the top, he takes me a few metres off to the side to see a marble vein at the surface. This part of the quarry has never been worked. On the ground, there are pieces of marble that have broken off naturally. Petros picks up one that would be just right for a figurine. He points to the plants and bushes and says their roots grow into fissures in the vein, and expand, and slowly pry off the chunks; it all happens naturally, he says, there was no need to quarry for small pieces in the Early Bronze Age. Quarrying didn't begin until much later, when large blocks of marble were needed for bigger sculptures.

We drive further and gain the ridge. Near a wind turbine rotating slowly in a gap, Petros pulls off the road. He wants to show me something. We walk to a small, single-story house with a large front porch, open to the sky. On it stands a 3-metre-high plaster cast of a classical Greek sculpture, a man holding a scroll. Next to it is a huge marble block from which the same man is emerging. This is the home of Giorgos Tsakiris. He makes reproductions of sculptures on commission.

Petros whistles into an open door, but no one emerges. He goes to the basement and brings out Giorgos to meet me. He's wearing a faded T-shirt with "Dream Team" printed on it. Giorgos invites us into his studio. It's full of sculptures of all periods and sizes, all in marble, all reproductions in various stages of completion. It takes a minute for my eyes to adjust to the indoor light, and then I see them – Cycladic figurines – the same ones they sell in the gift shop at the Museum of Cycladic Art in Athens. On shelves and worktables I see plaster casts and wood templates of the figurines. There are a dozen or so figurines on a table, all identical, all in white marble, and another dozen on the floor, leaning against a wall. There are three large, white marble slabs with outlines of the same figurine traced on them. They are traced head to toe, in tight rows, like cookies ready to be cut from rolled-out dough. There are another two slabs like this leaning against a wall. Some of the figurines on a shelf have broken legs. Giorgos says he had problems with that batch. I turn and find more figurines of a different style lying on their backs on another table, waiting to be finished. Then I see two roughed out versions of a much larger figurine, leaning against a wall, the marks of Giorgos's power tools still visible on the surface, like ripples in wet sand. Petros points out several large Cycladic bowls roughed out of square blocks of marble.

Giorgos says, with Petros translating, that he has made thousands of figurines. He's been doing this for the museum for more than 20 years. I ask Petros to ask Giorgos if he likes the figurines, if he finds them inspiring in any way. I can tell Petros is reluctant. They converse in Greek, then the answer comes: "not really." Petros explains: it's just a job. Giorgos prefers making reproductions of classical Greek sculptures.

Petros says that Giorgos uses marble from mainland Greece to make the figurines. The marble on Tinos is not the right colour, and the marble quarried on Naxos is course-grained. Giorgos doesn't want to have to travel to Naxos and ask farmers if he can pick up pieces of marble from their land, so he has white, fine-grained marble shipped to him from a quarry on the mainland. Then he ships his reproductions back to the mainland for sale in the museum. Giorgos says he can make a figurine in two or three days. He makes them in batches, assembly-line fashion. He does it all with power tools, except for hand finishing. He says he prefers making larger figurines because he can make them faster and they are less fragile, so there is less risk of breakage.

Another stop, another marble factory. A large dog on a chain barks as we pull in, but it barely rises from the dirt. Petros chides it, says it's "crazy." (Perhaps the noise has driven it insane?) I follow Petros into a hanger-like building where a man is grinding marble with a screaming power tool. He wears neither ear plugs nor eye protection, just a thick plastic bib to protect his clothes from the spraying water. The man Petros is looking for is not there. Petros heads into the yard, tape-measure in hand, looking through rough blocks of marble, some as big as a car. There is machinery everywhere – a forklift, an earth mover, a crane. Petros can't find what he's looking for. The museum wants him to build an exhibit that will recreate a traditional quarry scene, using four or five enormous marble blocks. Finding the right size blocks that he can assemble inside the museum is proving to be a headache. He says we'll have to go to this factory's quarry, to see if there are any suitable blocks up there.

The way up is all deep ruts and potholes. The road switch-backs up the side of a mountain. Boulders have been pushed to the side by earth-moving machines. We bottom-out occasionally, but Petros presses on, choosing his route carefully, keeping the tires on high ground, coming to a complete stop sometimes before inching forward. The road slashes through fields of purple heather. Petros says all the land on Tinos is privately owned, so the company pays the landowner for the right to quarry. This landowner still keeps goats and bees, but Petros points out abandoned terraces. He says barley was once grown here.

The quarry is a vast site just below the summit of the mountain. Clouds are brushing the peak, the wind raising swirls of sand and marble dust. No one is around. There is machinery everywhere: a dump truck, an earth mover, a high-lift loader, their tires all scarred with cuts from the rocks. There are oil drums marked BP, battered fuel tanks, and a padlocked shipping container marked "Sweden." There are old tires on the ground, and coils of hoses and cables.

Petros calls me. He's standing at the mouth of a two-storey high cavity in the side of the mountain, an abscess eaten away by machines. Exposed before us are the folds in a vein of marble. The folds look like huge waves arrested in motion, like breakers rolling onto a beach, though what we are actually seeing are cross-sections of the tops of massive folds of marble. Petros calls them "sarcophagus." Some of the folds look like raw bread dough, sagging under its own weight. There are folds on top of folds. There are gaps between some of them, so large you could crawl back into the womb of the earth. The surface of the marble is stained red and covered in a dusting of red soil, but where it has been scratched by machines or cracked open, it is brilliant white, glittering like the sea in sunlight.

At first I can't read what's in front of me, until Petros gestures with sweeps of his arm, showing me the angle and direction of the vein. He shows me the face, the head, and the *morello* of the vein, and his hand rises and falls like a boat on a wave as it traces the folds. It looks a jumble, like the sea in a storm, but slowly I begin to grasp the bigger picture, the unfathomable motion in geologic time that pushed this vein upward from the depths below.

I am the woman of the rock
I am the gift of the sea

Petros scrambles up a three-metre-high pile of rock debris and peers into another opening in the side of the mountain. He points to the continuation of the vein in the dim light. But I am suddenly conscious of the suffocating weight of unstable red earth above us. We are standing below a ten-metre-high cliff of freshly exposed and undercut mountainside. I walk away and turn around and look up. I see an old dry stone wall at the edge of the clawed-away mountainside, ready to topple down onto where we were standing. Petros seems unconcerned. He leads the way to another, nearby excavation. Inside are more folds of marble. But here there are also small stalactites dripping down onto the marble from a layer of stone above.

He takes me to another spot in the face of the mountain, and shows me where the quarry workers are in the process of cutting an enormous block of marble out of the vein. A block has already been taken, leaving a smooth white surface. The block they are preparing to take out next is as tall as a one-story house; I can't tell how far back it goes. Petros shows me the holes they have drilled into the stone in several places, and explains how steel cables with diamond teeth are inserted into the holes and drawn around in a circular loop through the marble to cut it away from behind and on the sides. Then the marble is levered up from below until it breaks free. Machines take it away.

In the middle of the quarry is a field heaped with marble. The pieces are all shapes and sizes, tumbled haphazardly, some on top of each other, many showing the marks of chains and drills. Some have one or two sides smooth and bare from the saws that cut them free; others are rough-hewn boulders, still covered in dirt, their inner beauty waiting to be revealed. Petros is not happy amidst all this devastation. I can see it in his face. He scrambles over the rocks like a goat, pulling out his tape measure, looking for the blocks he needs. I can't keep up with him. It reminds me of crossing a talus slope; one slip and you break a leg.

I wander off to the perimeter of the quarry and look over an old stone wall at the fields that slope away on the other side. There are abandoned terraces, and the ground is overgrown with heather. A few hundred metres away, and a little further below, I see another large plot of land ripped open; a quarry has been started there, too.

"We are pirates!" Petros snarls, spinning the wheel of the Toyota to keep us out of the ruts on the way down. At first I don't understand. Then I realize he's talking about the way we take marble from the earth now. It's all machines, he says. The quarry employs only two or three men. This is why his son doesn't want to follow in his father's footsteps: it's horrible to work in these quarries, and even this brief visit has upset Petros. He can't help comparing the devastation we have just seen to the modest, hand-worked quarry we visited earlier, that employed many more men, that reverberated with the sound of chisels and hammers, not roaring diesel engines and drills, that made quarrying marble a dignified trade. I remember those two crosses I saw lying on their sides in the stone shelter: requiem for a time when men worked close to the earth with simple tools. I ask Petros if the company will cover up the quarry when they are finished and restore the mountainside to its original contour. By law they have to, he says. "But when the quarry is finished, the company is finished. Better to leave it in the ground!"

Observe: he picks up a stone. It is raw marble, white and flat. He kneels beside a boulder of grey marble. He picks up another piece of marble to use as a hammer and sets to work. He's down on one knee, his feet bare in sandals. He holds the piece of white marble against the boulder with one hand, and quickly and steadily begins hammering the edge of it with the other stone. He is roughing out the shape of a Cycladic figurine. He is doing what someone would have done 4,000 years ago, using a stone tool to shape a piece of marble picked up off the ground. Cars speed by on the main road, a neighbour calls a greeting to him in passing, but in the work going on before my eyes we could be in the Early Bronze Age.

   No words.
   Watch.

     After –
        Words.

Petros works quickly, facing into the sun, oblivious to the glare. I am mesmerized by his intentness. He holds the emerging figurine against a sharp edge on the boulder, with only a centimetre or two protruding beyond the edge. He varies this amount, and the angle of stone against boulder, continuously. Using the other chunk of marble, he taps at the edge of the figurine, but never at right angles to the face of it. He is chipping off flakes at a 45-degree angle, first from one side of the *morello*, then from the other, leaving a pointed *morello*, as if the edge of the figurine were a dull blade. He continually alternates sides, moving quickly around the figurine. Around and around, first one face of the stone up, then the other, alternating back and forth, constantly adjusting his blows and the position and angle of the figurine. He works quickly, perhaps two or three strikes a second, with great precision. Chips fall off with almost every blow, and each seems to achieve his purpose. The chips are small, the size of peas, or smaller. His hands and jeans and shirt quickly become covered in fine white powder. Small chips fly at his face, but he doesn't falter. When the rough outline of the figurine is there, the edges roughly pointed, he suddenly adjusts the angle of stone on boulder and goes around it again, knocking the point off, leaving a flat edge all around.

With a raw figurine in hand, he begins using other techniques to work on parts of it. Sometimes he rubs the edges of the figurine directly against the boulder, taking off rough spots. Other times he puts down the stone he is using as a hammer and taps the figurine directly on the block. I expect chips to come off the block, but they only come off the figurine. He is demonstrating what he told me earlier: that when you know marble, you can see which part of the stone is hard and which is soft; you can see fracture lines and cracks and impurities; and with this knowledge, you can see the effect of each blow before you make it. He is working the marble figurine with two other pieces of marble, yet almost all the chipping and breaking is happening on the piece he wants to shape. His tools are barely affected.

I see that Petros concentrates his energy when he works: his hammering is controlled; his strokes are short; his hand moves only a few centimetres back and forth; but the force of his blow is powerful. He reminds me of a Tai chi teacher I once had: small motion, small visible movement, powerful effect. The power is internal, the teacher used to say, it begins with the breath. Petros grunts as he works; the sound is a sharp exhalation of breath.

> *hit chip turn*
> *hit chip turn*
> *hit chip turn*

hit chip turn

This is all happening fast. Petros is ignoring me and my scribbling, wholly focussed on his work. He puts down the piece of marble he has been using as a hammer, looks at the ground beside him, and picks up another stone. He tries using it to hammer, but after a few blows throws it away. He resumes tapping the figurine directly on the boulder, but he's not satisfied with the effect. There is a tiny protrusion he wants to chip off next, but he is having trouble. He gets up, looks around, and comes back with another stone. He hits a couple of blows with it, but it is too soft. He gets up again and walks to another marble boulder, this one green. He approaches it knowingly. He finds a part of the boulder that suites his needs – a particular shape and sharpness – and starts to work again, alternately tapping or rubbing the figurine against the boulder vigorously. I see what he is trying do. He wants to cut further into the hollow where the neck meets the shoulder. It's one thing to chip around the outside of a convex curve; that he did easily, on the first boulder. The problem is how to chip deeper into a concave curve. But he is not exactly chipping now: he is striking and grinding in one continuous motion. It's like watching a baker knead bread, first slamming the dough down onto a board, then extending the downward motion into a forward roll with the heel of the hand. Petros is bringing the nape of the neck down lightly onto a protruding edge of the boulder and rolling the energy, the force of the strike, out into a short grind along the edge of the boulder. The edge of the figurine is grinding now more than chipping, and there is fine white powder accumulating on the darker boulder. But this, too, is not working entirely to his satisfaction, though the outline of the figurine is now clear. He walks quickly past me to a nearby wall. He takes a stone off the top and lays it on the ground and prepares to make another attempt, but suddenly stops, and turns to me. "This is *chalazías*, quartz. If I had a bigger piece I could work better."

He shows me the figurine he has roughed out. There is a head and neck, and broad rounded shoulders tapering to a blunt end where the feet will be. The legs are a solid mass, the arms are not yet discernible. It looks like a body wrapped in a shroud. About 15 minutes have passed since he started. He waits for my questions.

I ask why he began chipping at angles, making a pointed edge first around the figurine, before breaking the point off. He says that by holding the figurine at an angle against the edge of the boulder, and striking it at an angle, the effect is like hitting the figurine simultaneously from both sides. He says the shock of the blow is reflected back at the figurine from the supporting stone underneath, and with practice you can control the force and the effect with great precision. He calls it "hitting from the bottom." I marvel at the fact that the chips that came off were all intended, and that despite the force of his blows, the slab did not break. "We have strong things in the marble, and we have softer things. When you know the stone, you can do this."

He leads the way back to his studio, carrying the figurine in one hand. He heads straight to a work table and sweeps the rubble and dust of the previous day's work onto the floor with the back of his hand. He grabs a large plastic sack half-filled with sand or marble dust from the floor and swings it up on to the table. He settles it down, tucks the open end underneath so it doesn't spill, and with the heel of his palm makes a depression in the middle. He lays the figurine there. He goes to another table and brings back a rough black stone. "This is emery." He picks up a steel hammer and breaks off a piece. He lays down the hammer and uses the emery as a tool. He uses it like a file, to smooth off the rough edges of the figurine. He puts down the small piece of emery, picks up the figurine, and lays the large piece of emery in the middle of the sack instead. Then he rubs the figurine against the emery. "We work many ways." The two pieces of stone – marble and emery – shift positions continually. Suddenly he puts down the stones and walks out of the studio. He returns with water in a makeshift bowl cut from the bottom of a plastic bottle. "Water helps," he says. "We work with water...." His voice trails off as he resumes his intent, silent work, dipping two fingers into the container and scooping water out onto the part of the marble he is working, washing away the marble "flour" and leaving the stone bare again.

Earth against earth
Wave against shore

He starts filing a vertical cleft between the legs of the figurine, and horizontal lines to outline the crossed arms. He is demonstrating the next phase of the work as an Early Bronze Age carver would have done it: after the rough shaping of the figurine, then anatomical details: nose, fingers, pubic triangle, toes. After about 10 minutes he stops, laughs, and shows me the figurine he has roughed out. "Maybe I'll make one someday!"

I ask about the water. "It cleans stone. Takes the dust away. It makes stone cold, so it cuts better. We have different stones. Some work better with water, some dry. Marble is better with water." He points to a large circular saw nearby, hanging vertically above a moveable steel bed. That saw uses water, too; the pool to supply it is just outside the studio.

We talk about the Early Bronze Age people and how they would have worked. He says it was the same way he just worked – first they chipped and shaped the *morello* and head of the stone – the head, bottom, and sides of the figurine. Why? Because those parts are harder to work. If there was breakage at that stage, the piece could be discarded without too much wasted effort. So, first the *morello* and head, and only then the face of the stone. The face is the softest, the easiest to work, and that's where the detail on the Cycladic figurines is found.

I ask him why so many of the Cycladic figurines are broken at the neck or the legs, but few through the torso. He explains: marble breaks at its thinnest part, even if struck at its thickest part. So if you drop a figurine, even if it lands on its middle, it will likely break at the neck or legs. He takes a pencil and draws on a polished slab of marble: he sketches a rough violin shape, two rounded thick ends with a narrow waist joining them. He points to the waist: if you want to break the marble here, he says, you hit there – pointing to the thickest part, at the end. Petros says the small Cycladic figurines were harder to make because of the fragility of the marble; larger figurines were less likely to crack while being worked. "Bigger is easier than smaller." (Almost all the figurines are small.)

We talk emery. It comes from the island of Naxos, 15 kilometres away. Until recently, emery was mined commercially there, for export. It's where the Early Bronze Age people got their emery, too. Emery is harder than marble, and heavier. Petros says that until the Second World War, marble-workers on Tinos used emery to work marble; there were no power grinders. Electricity didn't come to some parts of the island until the mid-1960s. All the time he was at the marble school in Pirgos, it was hand work. He says you can use emery in many ways. He says you can cut a shape into a piece of emery stone so that the emery becomes a template for the shape you want in the marble.

We talk tools. He says the Early Bronze Age sculptors would have made tools from materials in their environment, unlike nowadays, when the carbide steel in his chisels comes from Italy. It wasn't that long ago, he says, that toolmakers, blacksmiths and marble workers worked alongside one other, as a team. Petros himself knows how to temper steel. The Early Bronze Age workers would have had to spend time making tools, and repairing and replacing them. Petros says they weren't just hitting or rubbing stone against stone. They would have made chisels from pieces of stone wedged into a wood handle. They would have made drills like that, too. He goes to a cabinet and takes out his favourite drill – an old, hand-operated drill, made of a single round shaft of wood with a groove around the middle. He explains: you put a bit into the end of the shaft; you press down on the other end of the shaft with one hand; and you spin the drill with a rope wrapped around the groove of the shaft and attached to a wooden bow, working it back and forth in a continuous sawing motion. No electricity, a single piece of wood, a bent branch for a bow, and a piece of rope: the Early Bronze Age carvers could have done the same, using a piece of emery as a bit. But he says the clefts between the legs of the Cycladic figurines, even the ones that go completely through the stone, were not made by drilling: you can see the tool marks; they were cut through with a piece of emery, rubbing it back and forth in the groove.

Finally, I ask if he thinks the tilted-back face of so many of the figurines, and their sometimes elongated heads, was because of the repetitive hand motion of the carvers as they filed down the face. He says no, the shape was a deliberate choice; they could have made the face flat. He says the Early Bronze Age carvers were skilled marble workers. The simple shape of the figurines was not because they couldn't carve more complex images. They were capable – look at the rare seated figurines that have been found, musicians holding harps or playing flutes. They were elaborately carved. They could do it, Petros insists, they had the skill. But those few exceptions aside, they chose to make *this* image – the female Cycladic figurine, arms folded, head tilted back, feet pointed. They chose to make it, again and again, for almost a thousand years.

There is no sound in death.
Only the wind on the hills of Louros Athalasou.
Chalandriani, Phyrroges, Zoubaria.

And the bleating of far-off goats.

Home is both land and body.

" – at home in your body."

The broken body sets free the dead.

I used to imagine my mother's death, and how I would feel. The surge of grief knocking me off balance. The absence in the city where she lives, the sudden lack of a pull to it, as if there were a failure of gravity and we lost our connection to Earth. Where would we be then, flying off into space, eternal wanderers? I used to imagine drifting north into less populated parts, driving down long stretches of road between nothing – trees, tundra, expanses of land. I know it is not empty, but my heart would be, an open space waiting to be populated.

Now I don't dare imagine her death. When I take her hand to steady her I feel the tiny bones, so delicate I could crack them in my grip. My love for her is diffuse. Often I do not feel it, though I know it is there. I don't want to talk of it. I am afraid to discover how deep it goes. A woman who knew me well said that I loved her most when I was far away. I don't want to talk of that, either. We are all exiles. We are never wholly and unwaveringly where we are, except in death.

Sea beat our body.

and the land will have names
and the names will be given by
what happened there –
what is remembered there –

    goat's bed
    widow's tear

Draw one line down. What word speaks of this? Arc? Sweep? Convex? It is as much absence, what is taken away from the stone.

Absence invites the hand.

It is absence that invites.

It was a time
when animals spoke
warnings were carried on the wind
clap of surf
a raptor's shadow
stone
clattering
from a height

All I have now is what I can imagine.

Grandfather used to play a game with me. I'd conceal a penny in one of my hands and he would take my clenched fists in his large, gentle hands, and wait. And watch me. He would always guess correctly, feeling me hold the secret tight.

They are like that, the figurines. Like clenched fists.[18]

None are perfect, or perfectly symmetrical. Each is unique. They are handmade, after all, and by different hands. All have a touch of the personal – a slight tilt or turn of the head, breast size and position, the shape of the belly, the angle of the arms.

Defining characteristics:
1. female
2. naked
3. arms folded over torso, left arm above right arm
4. blank face, pronounced nose
5. head tilted back
6. feet drooping

they wear nothing, hold nothing[19]

> Structure – ?
>
> hero on a quest to solve a mystery
> goes through various episodes
> meets different people –

Transcript: Lesley Fitton, archaeologist.[20]

It's interesting: you used the word 'mysterious'. I was talking to another archaeologist and he said, "Don't use the word 'mysterious' with archaeologists. We don't like that word." How did he put it? That it's sort of –

– a failure of interpretation? I'm not so sensitive about that. If I could answer all the questions unequivocally I'd say there's nothing mysterious about them, but of course there is. And it is partly due to a failure of archaeology, in the sense that the excavation history of the Cyclades has been a troubled one. Our early excavations were not well documented. And then, by the time we get into the 20th century, there was a huge problem with looting. So in a sense there's been a failure of – I wouldn't say it's just archaeologists – it's a failure of humanity, really. It's a sad thing.

Bones were tossed aside, left to decay in the open air. Archaeologists still can't say whether the figurines were buried with the bodies of men or women. Or children.

More than 80 per cent (some estimates go as high as 90 per cent) of the figurines in the world are unprovenanced. We don't know where they came from, or even whether they're authentic. Some forgeries are so good, even the experts have been fooled.

Greece's state museums, the National Archaeological Museum in Athens and smaller state-run museums on the islands, hold only figurines that are provenanced, from authorized excavations. But unprovenanced figurines are held in museums and private collections all around the world.

One way Greece tried to stem the illicit export of looted objects, and repatriate those that had already been smuggled out, was to encourage wealthy Greek citizens to start their own private collections. One such collection was started in the early 1960s by Nicholas and Dolly Goulandris, using money from the family shipping business. They amassed the largest private collection of unprovenanced figurines in the world and built the Museum of Cycladic Art, in Athens, to exhibit their collection and encourage research.[21] This, too, is not without controversy: some scholars argue that private collectors unwittingly promote looting, and that publishing scholarly research about unprovenanced artifacts enhances their market value, driving up prices and fueling the trade in looted objects and forgeries.

She's in the room, but I can't see her. This is what it must feel like when someone dies. This is what it must feel like when someone goes off to war. Yes, that's what it's like: I'm waiting for her to return.

    Moon of the Full Belly
    Moon of the Dark Sea
    Moon of the Birds Leaving

    Moon of the Long Night
    Moon of Hunger, Moon of Sorrow

    Moon of the Birds Coming Back to Us

Moon of the New Lambs
Moon of the Full Net

Moon of the Laughing Child[22]

From the moment of stooping to pick up a stone, the figurines required continuous attention to bring them into the world. They embody attention.

What remained after the rubbing of stone against stone: residue, a mingling of dusts.

White

milk of the goat
milk of the woman
river bed sand

sea foam
sea-turned stone
throat of the bird that follows

Their arms are crossed, their faces blank. Why am I drawn?
Abstract beauty, certainly. The beauty of shape and line, of pure form.

But there is something more.

Imagine a god named Sky.

What words do we have now to speak to the gods? What words join us to the stars and the sea, to the animals and plants by whose dying we live? We name them, but they are not sung. Our language is clotted. We do not remember. Our books hold memory, but we do not. We have forgotten how to sing to the dead.

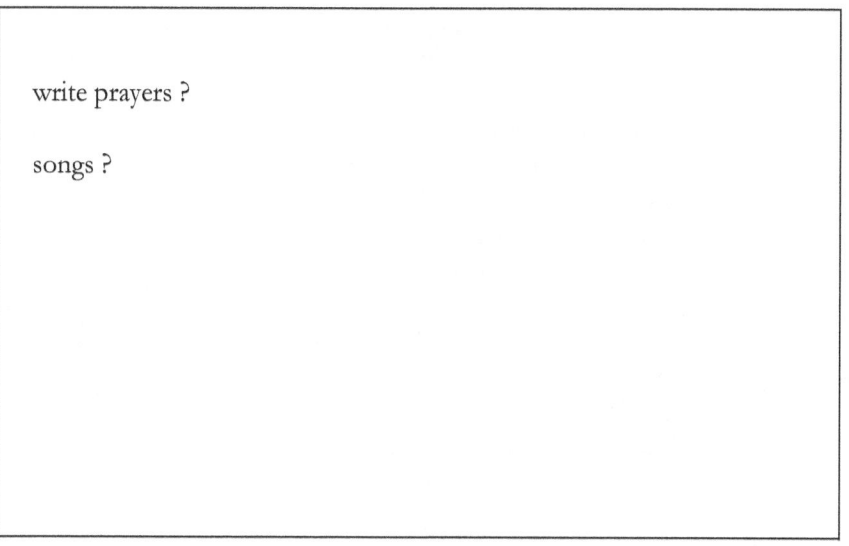

There was a time when one could write, "The land didn't know him. It stared back at him, blank and prickly."

But that time is past.

The ceiling is vaulted, the floors are wood planks. My spirit lifts with the arches and the light. A tall window looks out to the mountains. In the morning, the window muntins and the security bars on the outside cast a long shadow on the floor that resembles the fretted neck of an old stringed instrument. It moves silently across the room. The vitrine in front of the window holds seven figurines. They are upright, one beside the other. I see their backs as I approach. They are in deep silhouette.

We have no hope but in you.[23]

During the 1950s and early 1960s, a small, uninhabited island called Keros became the talk of archaeologists and collectors when several hundred Early Bronze Age artifacts said to come from the island flooded the international antiquities market. They became known as "The Keros Hoard." Estimates of the number of figurines in the hoard range from about 250 to 350. All of the objects were illicitly taken from Keros and smuggled out of Greece by a network of middlemen and unscrupulous art dealers.[24] There is no way of knowing whether all the objects were in fact from Keros; we have only the looters' and dealers' word to take for that, and as Keros assumed almost mythic status it's not unlikely that objects looted from other islands were claimed to be from Keros, to fetch a higher price. But there was no doubt that Keros has been heavily plundered: a site called Kavos on the western tip of the island was ransacked. As word spread, and as museums and private collectors around the world continued buying the objects, looters continued going to Keros.

In 1963 the Greek authorities sent an archaeologist, Christos Doumas, to the island to see what was there and to rescue what he could. Doumas found pieces of figurines, pottery, and bone scattered over the ground and buried at varying depths in the soil. He also found traces of buildings both at Kavos and on a tiny islet called Dhaskalio that faces the site, only 50 metres offshore. Doumas surmised that the islet had once been connected to Keros by a strip of land. He put forward the theory that the looted site on Keros had been a cemetery for a settlement on the islet, and that the cemetery had been destroyed at some point by a geological upheaval – an earthquake, a landslide, or subsidence. Evidence of an upheaval could still be seen: large boulders had rolled down the mountainside. Four years later, a second rescue excavation was carried out by Photeini Zapheiropoulou and Kostas Tsakos. They found more broken figurines and other artifacts at the looted site at Kavos. But neither excavation found graves.

Archaeologists began wondering whether there had in fact been a cemetery on Keros. That doubt prompted new questions. Cycladic figurines were usually found in graves. If there was no cemetery, why were there so many figurines on Keros?

For the next 30 years, theories piled up and evolved. First, two German archaeologists, Olaf Höckmann and Jürgen Thimme, suggested that Kavos may have had a special religious significance. A British archaeologist, Colin Renfrew, went further, suggesting that Kavos may have functioned as a religious sanctuary where Early Cycladic people intentionally smashed objects. Doumas accepted Renfrew's theory and went a step further, suggesting that the bones of the dead and their accompanying grave goods may have been brought to Keros from other islands.

In 1987-88, joint teams of Greek and British archaeologists excavated again. They found more pieces of figurines, pottery, and other objects, but still no graves. Lab analysis showed that most of the pottery had come from other islands, leading the researchers to postulate that there had been a settlement on Keros and that it may have been an important maritime trading centre.[25]

In the 1990s, The Museum of Cycladic Art in Athens acquired a sizeable number of the Keros Hoard figurines after a private Swiss collector who had been holding them put them up for auction at Sotheby's in London and New York. Peggy Sotirakopoulou, an archaeologist working at the museum, began an exhaustive study of the Keros Hoard figurines, both the ones at the museum and all the pieces she could locate in private collections and museums around the world. Lab analysis showed that the marble used to make most of them had come from several places on Naxos, though some had come from Keros itself. Two pieces of figurines from the private Swiss collection were found to match provenanced figurines from authorized excavations, leading Sotirakopoulou to conclude that at least some of the looted figurines in The Keros Hoard had indeed come from Keros.[26] But she could add nothing conclusive to the speculation about why so many broken figurines had been found on the island.

In another attempt to find answers, a major, three-year excavation by British and Greek archaeologists began in 2006, led by Colin Renfrew and supported by experts in palaeoethnobotany, archaeometallurgy, geology, and radiometric dating. They made a major discovery – another site at Kavos, untouched by the looters, its archaeological record intact. It was a large pit not far from the looted site. In it, in strata going down two metres, the archaeologists found more than 550 pieces of figurines and more than 2,300 pieces of marble bowls and other vessels. But no bones or teeth were found. Nor were there any of the ornaments and other things typically found in Early Cycladic graves. The researchers looked inside fissures in the ground near the site, which others had speculated might be a collapsed cave. They found no bones or artifacts inside. They concluded that there was no cemetery, at least not at the site they had discovered. They surmised that there was no cemetery at the nearby looted site either, but the devastation there was so bad they'd never know for sure.[27]

What they could prove, through lab analysis, was that the fragments of figurines found in the pit had been deliberately broken. But no matching parts were found. From that the archeologists surmised that the figurines had been broken on other islands, and that some, but not all, of the pieces had then been taken to Keros.

The team also excavated on the islet of Dhaskalio. There they uncovered settlement walls made of white marble from Naxos, and a circular enclosure on the summit containing hundreds of round white pebbles brought from Ano Kouphonisi. And they found figurines. But in striking contrast to Keros, none of the figurines on Dhaskalio were broken, and all of them were schematic figurines. Not a single, folded-arm figurine was found on the islet. The researchers determined that the settlement periodically accommodated up to 400 visitors, but that only around 20 people lived there year round.

Renfrew and his colleagues concluded that Dhaskalio and the western tip of Keros had been joined by a narrow causeway during the Early Bronze Age, and that together they had served as a sanctuary, attracting people on pilgrimages from all over the Cyclades. Rituals were performed there, involving broken objects. People had travelled there repeatedly for 450 years, starting around 2750 BC. That made it the oldest sanctuary in the world accessible only by sea.[28] More Cycladic figurines are now documented as coming from Keros than from all the previous archaeological excavations in the Cyclades put together. And yet, Renfrew believes that more figurines may have been stolen from Keros by looters prior to 1963 than have been recovered by all the archaeological excavations there since.[29]

    something spoke through you
    and was taken by the wind

    now it is silence you want us to hear

I am the woman of the rock[30]
I am the bones of the land

Another way of remembering: the "winter counts" of the Dakota nation. Each winter was given the name of an event that happened that season, and then the name was recorded as an ideogram.

Many-women-died-in-childbirth-winter.[31]

If the figurines were a representation of death, then smashing the figurine might have been a ritual resistance to death, an affirmation of life in the face of the inevitable.

Equally, the ritual breaking may have been a symbolic severing of bonds with the one who had died.

Either way, death was pushed back.

Peindre, non la chose, mais l'effet qu'elle produit.[32]

Only the hand knows stone.

Only the hand finds the waist.

> Write in fragments, as if the text has missing parts?
> As in Sappho?
>
> Use dots or other typographic marks to signal missing words and lines?
>
> Armand Schwerner says this way of writing offers "ways out of closure."
>
> Schwerner, quoted in Rothenberg, ed., *Technicians,* 475.

According to Frazer, in *The Golden Bough,* two principles of thought underlay magic.[33] One principle he calls "imitative magic." The magician sees in nature that like produces like, and infers that he can produce any effect he wants by imitating it. Frazer says this kind of magic was mostly used to hurt an enemy. But it was also used constructively. For example, some "primitive" societies helped women in childbirth by giving her an image of a child to hold in her lap, or suckle. By the same thinking, imitating stillness would produce stillness. Are the figurines meant that way? Did holding them bring stillness? Were they given to the agitated, the distraught, the grieving?

The other principle that Frazer identifies is what he calls "contagious magic." Things that were once in contact with one other continue to act upon one other at a distance. There is a "secret sympathy" between them, even though physical contact has been severed. Similarly, whatever is done to an object will affect equally the person with whom the object was once in contact. By this thinking, breaking the figurine would affect the one who possessed or cared for the figurine. But, equally, did a figurine remain forever in sympathy with the seam of marble from which it was taken, experiencing rain, sun, the passing of hooves? Was the figurine seen as a wanderer, living for a while among people, before one day returning to the earth, to be reunited with the bones of the land that emerge as outcrops of marble on the hills? Was that why the figurines were buried?

> *I feel hooves —*
> *I hear bees —*
>
> *in the night sky I see my way home*

and the eyes are given
that they may see

> *we gathered the animals close*
> *we brought grasses into the house*
> *we dug holes (deep holes)*
> *for our tubers and our mast*

now, heather grows on the graves
sweetening the air
for the hunter's guns.

He opens a book and reads.

There are no half-formed languages, no underdeveloped or inferior languages. Everywhere a development has taken place into structures of great complexity. People who have failed to achieve the wheel will not have failed to invent and develop a highly wrought grammar. Hunters and gatherers innocent of all agriculture will have vocabularies that distinguish things of their world down to the finest details.[34]

Jerome Rothenberg, in *Technicians of the Sacred*, writes that "primitive" poetry is inseparable from music, dance, painting, and myth. Poetry is spoken or chanted or sung, and in the act of doing so, one line will be repeated "until its burden has been exhausted."[35] And then the poem moves on.

Rothenberg also writes that "primitive" poetry achieves its unity by imposing a "key" on the world – a sound, a rhythm, a name, a gesture – something consistent around which everything else can be inconsistent. Meanings can change, forms can be open, causality abandoned, contradictions allowed, yet there's a sense of unity surrounding the poem, a solidarity of all life. The poem's purpose, Rothenberg says, is to overcome doubt.[36]

The figurines work like that, like a key, like a one-line poem repeated indefinitely. The form was imposed on the world. Everything around it might be hard to pin down. But the folded arms, the upturned face, these erase doubt.

> Be still in death.
> Be among us ever in our hearts.
> Sit beside us at the fire.
> Do not trouble us with complaints.
> Do not drive malice among us.
> Be still in our hearts
> And we will ever be with thee.

Did the figurines provide a symbolic vehicle for addressing death? Through them, could people converse with, and hold, their departed? Did painting the figurines give the departed life again: eyes to see, colour in the skin? Did giving the figurines a place in the home reassure the dead that they still had a place among the living?

> *we anoint thee with colour*
> *we wrap thee in the skins of our animals*
> *we bathe thee in the sea*

> dissociate, not associate –
>
> is this the way back?

> Two competing voices, or impulses – the rational and the irrational?
>
> The rational seeks explanation, accumulates facts, makes notes.
> It speaks *of*.
>
> The irrational speaks *through*.
>
> Are there other voices beside the human –
> the sky, the sea, the land, the stone?

More words than he knows what to do with sometimes.

Rothenberg writes that the basic function of poetry in preliterate societies is this: "something has been sighted and stated and set apart."[37] From there, one can build structures and visions. But it starts, he says, with a single image, set apart.

The figurines are that, a single image, stated in stone and set apart. All the structures that were elaborated upon the image are gone, the story that grew up around it, the rituals and songs – gone. We have only the image. And we cannot see behind the image, cannot see the prior "thing sighted."

> causing trees to bear fruit
> causing trees to bear fruit again, the following year

Frazer says stone was considered "steadfast." One would swear on stone. Magical properties were attributed to different stones. One would lay one's stone beside another person's stone to transfer the magical properties from one to the other.[38]

We still pick up stones.

Some figurines are believed to have been carved from stones washed up on the beach.

> enemy or friend
> both approached from the sea
>
> the return of loved ones –
> from the sea

It occurs to him that they must have had different words for the surface of the sea. But how could he enter that knowledge? Personification of the sea was unavailable to him, now, adjectives like angry, morose, all the anthropomorphism of past generations – gone.

But to them, who saw gods below the waves – and not just saw, but knew – to them, the sea spoke.

I see the language of the form. I see the form itself as a language. But I cannot hear the words.

In my mind, I see the perfect arrangement of words on a page, words that will give voice to the form. But it is an illusion. It cannot exist. Meaning cannot be resurrected outside of language.

> The land is an open grave.
> Soil, the dust of bones –
>
> Thyme grows sweet upon it.
>
> Honey glows in the jar.

My mother is old now. It is hard for me to leave her for long.

I don't live with her. I have lived in a succession of rooms, up flights of stairs – hardly a home for an elderly woman.

I am in constant motion, but always in orbit. I hear her calling me.

In truth, it is me, calling her.

He meets a woman (perhaps). She is a painter (perhaps). She is deaf and mute. She paints with oils, landscapes empty of people. They are lonely, he writes on the pad, and pushes it across the table. That is my life, she writes, and pushes it back. He cannot draw, but he makes sketches in his notebook, ink on lined pages. He shows them to her, dismissing them with a laugh and an exaggerated sweep of his hand. He takes the pad and writes, They help me remember – and pushes it across to her. She does not reply.

squalls overnight

dogs yap at the edge of town
smelling kill

men idle their Honda 50s, smoking

goats forage in the rubble

Everything is preparation. He is always laying in stores – of sleep, of fitness, of sensibility. His one task (he tells himself) is to cultivate sensibility, and the rest will follow.[39] And for that he sits with the figurines in the museum, doing nothing but looking and listening and willing his chest to open, and in so opening, he hopes, fill with them, until they spill out of him later in words.

More examples of "contagious magic" from Frazer:[40]

The placenta was seen as the sibling or double of the child. Some threw the placenta into water, so the child would learn to swim well. Some put it in a pot with ashes and left it in a tree, to watch over the child as the child grew up.

The umbilical cord, hung in a tree, would ensure a boy became a good hunter. A girls' chord might be buried beside the hearth.

gather the blood, from the ground
the clots in the dust

take them to the cliff

throw them over
at the rising tide

Injuring a footprint would injure the foot that made it. Hunters injured the print of the animal they were pursuing; or placed charms on the print, to slow it down; or gathered a handful of dust from the print, and threw it in the air, so the animal would fall to the ground like the dust.

My fingertips moved over her.

Different voices – ?

voice of the marble
voice of the stones that were rubbed against the marble
voice of the woman in the stone
voice of the carver
voice of the "owner" of the figurine, alive, and then later in the grave

images see with the eyes of those who see them[1]

Walter Murch, speaking of early photographic portraits, says they were once-in-a-lifetime photographs. Dressed in their Sunday best, looking directly at the camera – this, he says, is how the people being photographed would be seen by future generations. He calls their blank expression "looking at eternity."[42]

    addressing stone –
    practice
    for our conversations
    with the dead

    hold them

        sea whispers beneath the cliff

A parallel story – ?

Someone has died, or is dying.

Or, I am anticipating someone's death.

Or, there is an accident, a sudden death.

Or, bodies wash up on the shore.

> Write one voice as a letter to someone, to be read after my death?
>
> But to whom – ?

The hills are bare. The forests that once covered the islands are gone, roots pulled out and burned, topsoil washed to the sea. The glare of light is intrusive. It burns skin and retina.

I remember the sudden relief stepping into a park planted with pine trees, the revelation: this was the way the light would have fallen, the way the ground would have yielded underfoot.

>   death comes from across the sea –
>   bodies, showing signs of torture
>
>   faces unrecognizable

The community's surplus energy went into making the figurines. That is a commonly held view of the art of subsistence cultures. We think of the energy as surplus because it is the energy the community allocated beyond what we regard as essential: food, shelter, clothing, weapons, tools. But that is our view. Perhaps the figurines were as essential as food.

It may also be true that it is only because the community lived amidst an abundance of food, in a temperate climate, that their arts developed. But no – think of the Inuit, in a harsh climate: even they allocate energy to art.

Even if making the figurines was the work of only a few craftsmen, someone had to feed and clothe them. In the late years of the culture, either the community no longer valued the figurines – a collapse of faith? a dislocation within society? – or the community's entire energy had to be diverted to physical survival.

Kastri, built in those late years, is writing on the land. The thick walls, the bastions facing the sea, the hilltop location – think of the effort required to carry food, water, and fuel up there.

What does Kastri mean? may be just as important to ask as, What do the figurines mean?

The figurines are a statement of something of supreme importance, something, we might say, on a different plane of existence. Let us call it the spiritual (though it's hard to imagine the Early Cycladic people using a word like *spiritual*, a word needed only when looking in). Let us call it a spiritual practice. What do the figurines tell us of this practice? Silence, stillness, renunciation – the folded arms hold nothing, not even a child, and the figurine itself was renounced by the living and interred in a grave, or broken and discarded. They seem to speak, too, of poise, of attentiveness. All this, we might say, is the "subject matter" of the figurines. The stylistic changes in the figurines down through the centuries might reflect an evolution in the society's religious rituals, or even in its collective spiritual attainment. But then, abruptly, it all came to an end. We could fantasize that the end of the practice of making figurines marked the final transcendence of the society spiritually, but this is at odds with the evidence, the fortifications, the bronze weapons. More likely, there was an abrupt sundering, something so cataclysmic that the society never recovered, spiritually or materially. Something came to an end.

He can smell it, on the air. The sunset is brilliantly coloured. He cannot read the headlines, but someone tells him: fires are burning, through groves and villages. There has been no rain in months. It will be remembered as the time of fire, the time of fear.

And I am looking through glass at them, looking through my own reflection in the glass, my eyes tired from squinting at labels, my feet swollen from the heat.

        and suddenly we were open
        everything falling suddenly open

        and open we fell
        into the sea

        and open we fell
        upon the lamb
        dripping with hunger

        throat songs we gave
        open songs
        praise songs

        the capstones pulled back

        open   to the sky

Literature, poetry in particular, is often self-referential – referring to the work of earlier poets. What, for a poet, lies further back than Homer?

What is a literature made of absence?

The beginning of writing is a wall behind which we cannot see.

We call their time "pre-history" but they had history. They could see back. They had a beginning they were sure of. They had a place in the song.

Emptiness can be a positive compositional and spiritual value. In medieval Japan, a time informed by Buddhism, large portions of a drawing were left white, empty. This was meant to set the human world of vanity, ambition, and violence against the spiritual emptiness of the cosmic order.[43]

The figurines were a kind of canvas on which people painted eyes, mouths, hair – the temporal stuff of human life and vanity. Now the paint is gone, and we are left contemplating the blankness, which is outside time. Only the "paint ghosts" are left – those rare faint outlines of eyes and other features we can discern on a few figurines, where the paint protected the marble from erosion. The Buddhists speak of big mind and small mind. The painted features were small mind, and the naked stone is now like big mind, the sea into which the wave subsides.

How does one write emptiness?

Example of *Red Beard*, by Akira Kurosawa – ?

The central character plays a small, often silent role, but those who come into contact with him are deeply affected by him. He is witness to transformations in those around him, but he himself does not change and we learn nothing about his past.

And so the figurines – ?

      bodies must be handled
      borne heavily to the grave

      women must wash them
      the limbs stiffening

      men must shoulder them
      the dead weight of them

      lifting   away

There is a sense, now, as I search for their meaning, that it is simply this: death, beyond which the individual body does not go.

And now, beyond which whole species do not go.

Our turn coming.

Words will not save us.

                                      Lie still
                                      Lie still

Czeslaw Milosz wrote that poetry depends on a "basic confidence" – "a sense of open space ahead of the individual and its human species."[44]

Where is that space now?

The land is burning. The fish stocks are depleted. The migratory birds are in decline. But still: hunters lean against their trucks, drinking raki, the dogs restless beside them.

We are so far from the gods. I held a figurine in my palm and could not understand why she was at rest there. I knew only that I knew nothing, nothing that could save us.

Basic narrative – ?

I journey through a dying world – the land ablaze, the sea fished out, war just over the horizon. I look for traces of Early Cycladic Culture, hints of meaning, clues to its demise. I find only graves, looted and silting in. Or places where graves have been plowed under, or built over. Archaeologists, overwhelmed, struggle to rescue the past from developers, from new roads and hotels. Conservators piece together shards. Their work is slow, the bulldozers work fast. And I am drawn again and again to a vitrine full of fragments, like bones stacked neatly in a genocide museum. I study the breaks, the raw marble revealed

inside the polished form. Whole figurines don't intrigue me as much as the raw breaks, phantom limbs of a vanished culture. Outside, fires burn on the hills. The forests that once covered the islands are gone. The tourists are in bars, drinking ouzo, racing through narrow streets on scooters, complaining about prices, looking for sex. And across the sea, not far, people are dying, their bodies torn by shrapnel, their skin burned by phosphorous.

> a cold view led us to this –
> staked ground
> numbers sprayed on old stone walls
> 57 58
> *the land now a broken whisper* [45]

Our earliest memories are like the figurines: we recognize ourselves in them, but remotely, at a distance. In my earliest memories, I do not speak: I am listening to the sound of my mother's voice.

The figurines come to us from a world that is mute. On the islands we can still hear the call of the sea birds and the repetitions of the waves. But everything else is gone: the sound the wind and the oak made, the sound the wind and the grasses made, the panting of wild animals.

> *the blue skin lay over us*
> *fish came to our net*
> *birds came to our net*
> *hearth smoke came to find us*

Should the protagonist be mute – ?

He writes notes, pushes them across the table, but does not speak.

How does one write in the face of extinction?

We have lost our memory.

We have forgotten our place.

We are armed and bewildered.

Three possibilities –

Write "miniatures" – micro-reports on the horrors of our age – no poetic artifice, no metaphor – everything condensed, detached, bulletin-like.

Write chants – "prehistory" songs – incantations.

Write a travel journal – amass fact and description – as if it matters, somehow – as if it will be of use to us, in the end.

People slip in.

Currents transport toxins.

We see too far over the edge of the world to ever be calm.

> The protagonist is aware of all the miseries and horrors happening around the world, through the internet and the media. He feels a weight of responsibility, it tempers his joy in living.
>
> Contrast: During the Early Bronze Age, news travelled only as fast as trading ships. They knew suffering, but not that it engulfed the world. They did not have to bear the weight of humanity's suffering, only their own.

Whence will renewal come to us, to us who have defiled and emptied the whole earthly globe? From the past alone, if we love it. [46]

> Model for oral narrative:
>
> ...., *they say*
> ....
> ....
> ...., *they say.*
>
> ....
> ....
>
> *This is where it ends.*

> Model for oral narrative: based on a story by Ghandl of the Qayahl Llaanas of Qaysun. Robert Bringhurst, *A Story as Sharp as a Knife: The Classical Haida Mythtellers and Their World* (Vancouver: Douglas & McIntyre, 1999), 32-44.

Look out from a hilltop.

In a world of natural forms, only the circle is perfect.

Eye of a fish. Eye of a child. Moon at its fullest.

Circles abound, but there are no straight lines.

Not even the edge of the world.

> *Invocare.*
>
> To call forth. To ask –
>
> For knowledge, for entry, for sign.
>
> As supplicants come, bewildered and weak.
>
> As men implore gods (– and women).

A similar effect, though inverse in scale: Henry Moore's female figures – the monumental white plasters in a room in the Art Gallery of Ontario.

In the beginning, Woman lay down beside Man, and there was life.

In the beginning, Woman lay down in the graves of Man, and there was life.

The form repeated, again and again, for centuries.
When it was exhausted (– what was exhausted?), the culture disappeared.

The disappearance of form and culture – which came first?
Does it make sense to talk of them separately?

        the departed cast shadow

        they do not submit to interrogation

Impossible to imagine a world where memory is unaided by writing, a world in which words cannot be secured against time and forgetting.

A world where sound is enough.

Impossible to imagine them not singing.

The galleries are quiet.

Marble picked up off the ground is rarely pure white. Pure white stones are found on the beach, polished by the waves, but what emerges in outcrops is in hues of white, stained by the earth.

Then the wonder: to pry loose a slab, and see the white gleam of crystals exposed for the first time.

Then the carver's work, each chip and abrasion uncovering more and more white, until the figurine emerges all white out of the stone.

And then buried. And all the colours of the earth colouring the white again, reclaiming it, marrying it to the other minerals, rains washing away all trace of the hand.

The earth reclaiming the stone.

>
> We have used up our time.
> It is the end of time.
>
> The land is turning to dust.

Plot possibilities – ?

Having stolen a figurine from a museum, I try to take it back to the Early Bronze Age cemetery from which it was taken.

Suspense: eluding the police, fooling the archaeologists, continuing my research while in possession of the stolen figurine. Will I be discovered?

I live with the figurine, holding it in my room, in the dark.

Do I succeed? –

I find the cemetery. I am alone. The graves are open. I rebury the figurine.

Or do I fail? – no cemetery found.

If I fail – drop the figurine overboard from a ferry?

Alternative plot: I go to Keros and break the figurine there, hoping for some illumination of the mystery.

Tonight, nothing.

to refine, to clarify, to intensify [47]

Like a traditional New Orleans funeral – ?

Sober out – meditation, reflections on the deceased.

Joyous return – improvisation, creation, renewal.

> In classical Greek theatre, the chorus functioned as a kind of on-stage audience. It responded to events, but could not influence them. It did not fully understand what was happening and why.
>
> Could I use a similar formulaic voice to allow nature to speak and respond, impotently, to changes wrought by humans on the environment?

Figurines observed in the Naxos museum:

Face pitted with erosion, like acne.

Stained rust-coloured all over, the colour of the soil. Or mottled in this colour. Or one side of the body coloured like this, the other side almost untouched. Some figurines appear dipped, others daubed, others lightly washed in colour.

Like swatches of burnt skin, dead and scaly.

Like dead flesh, ugly deep dead: some brown, some grey, others grey-turning-black.

Squirrelly lines of incrustation, like varicose veins, or like worms under the skin.

Like a burn victim: the entire face and body seared a rusty brown.

Lightly speckled in black, like mold on a wall.

Like scabs before they fall off, crusty and thick and dry.

Like purplish black death coming to the surface from inside the body, the skin still smooth and almost translucent.

A whole torso turned faint grey-yellow, with mottling of darker grey.

Creamy yellow-white, the crystals of the marble so small and the surface so finely polished it looks like marzipan. Or finely textured shortbread, heavy on the butter, soft to the touch.

Like a battle wound healing, but the disfiguration permanent, the eye and part of the cheek pitted and brown.

The whole body a sickly, chalky grey, with spots of black creeping up the back and neck and head and around the sides of the face.

Is this what gangrene looks like, black spreading, the flesh eaten away?

Erosion on one shin like a lesion, a slight cavity, rough and grey.

All shades of reddish-brown. One figurine so brown it looks almost "brown-skinned," with a lighter swatch on the right thigh, as though pigment were missing there.

Sometimes the discolouration is darker at the feet and lower legs, fading to lighter at the head, as if the figurine had been dipped in colour and stood up to dry.

Sometimes ugly chip scars: one or two strikes of the shovel or trowel ringing the stone, then the excavator dropping his tool, dropping to his knees in the dirt, and proceeding by hand: a chip missing from the bridge of the nose, white scars on a wrist, a wounded thigh.

Endless variations on white, like looking through all the hues of white in a line of paint samples: who imagined white could have so many shades? – eggshell, cream, chalk, cloud. How do we name white and its illnesses? – jaundiced, grey, bruised, pale, bloodless, deathly.

I keep seeing bones.

I keep seeing ossuaries. Rwanda. Cambodia.

> *Left lower leg of a figurine.*
>
> *Part of the right leg of a figurine.*
>
> *Part of the torso and thighs of a figurine.*[48]

The pleasure we take in stacking things up.

Time is the pulse of story. Plots move forward in time. But here there is no time – the grave, the stone, the fragments in glass vitrines.

Here is stillness. Here is death, the absence of time.

> *The foot is preserved. The legs were integral to the ankles.*[49]

a shudder staggers the ship

All those appointments, where I asked questions. All those hours spent looking, scribbling, sketching. Drawn to something I couldn't name. My inquiry became a kind of duty I needed to fulfill. I performed well, filled notebooks, worried archaeologists with my endless scribbling. ("Did you ask Yannis all these questions, too?") All this was a game of sorts, though I was earnest in my inquiries. I was playing at gathering facts, clinging to facts, all the while waiting for someone to let slip the words that would allow me to slip inside.

Time passes slowly in the winter night
darkness a land to wait out —

Imagine the hearth fires, edged with stone, kernels of light and warmth in the damp narrow confines of the settlement, the walls dripping, the sea black and heaving nearby.

Imagine goats bleating in low-roofed pens, babies crying, the thud of pestles, sentries talking at the gate.

And the wind, ceaseless, driving rain horizontal, skittering loose ends, everyone, beast and human, nervous, straining to hear.

And yet I think I only see the surface of things.[50]

Letters to my mother —

Or to the figurines —

Elegies to the missing dead?

I look at the postcards that I bought in the museums.

I think of sending them to her, one a month, starting with the fresco of a bird leaping off a branch.

I will send them without words.

She asked for no words.

Abandonment is a foreshadowing of death.

> Make Petros, the marble-worker, my guide — as Virgil was to Dante?

        vertical column
        geologic strata
        sedimentary processes
        isotope values
        grain size
        translucence

dead men, naked [51]

The point of view should not only be human.

In aboriginal cosmologies, animals, the land, even inanimate objects are sentient.

We have forgotten how to sing.

Our throats are hoarse with lost memory.

Burial Event:[52]

[Call and response. Repeat indefinitely, with gestures.]

       Bury the tail of a fish.
                          – On the beach.
       Bury the foot of a goat.
                          – On the hill.
       Bury the stone.
                          – In the river.
       Bury a feather.
                          – In the wound of a tree.

[gestures:]

On the beach: Hands in front, waist height, palms down. Start with hands touching, then open arms wide, like smoothing a tablecloth.

On the hill: Point to the hill.

In the river: Palms together, like gassho, but horizontal, pointing away. Then extend arms forward and open, parting water.

In the wound of a tree: Open right hand chops the palm of the left hand, once.

        They ask silence
                arrest

        The cessation of discourse

        Only our eyes moving
                tracing the line

Does breaking the body release the spirit?
Was that the motive for smashing the figurines?

The ritual killing of objects has been practised by humans from time immemorial. It still is – statues of the once powerful are pulled down, smashed, decapitated, buried.

There was a time when victors broke the bones of their slain enemies.[53]

The living are in struggle with the dead.

Frazer called it "carrying out death."[54]

Could it have happened like this – ?

a winter voyage:

the bones removed from the hillside cemetery
taken to Keros
making room for new life

returning from Keros, rituals must be performed
ensuring spring returns –

the winter sea voyage a defiance of death
a test for the son

sailing to Keros, bearing bones
his boat is not welcome at other settlements
even in a storm

.....

before departure, a ceremony:

girls (virgins) carry the dead woman's figurine to the boat
her son carries her bones, wrapped in her favorite skin
the village gives him supplies

if he sinks en route, death is drowned
if he makes it to Keros, the bones are left, the figurine smashed

either way, a place is made for new life

if he returns with a song, so much the better –

Two voyages – ?

First, to Keros with the bones – the son's final conversation with his mother – a night voyage, a defiance of death, a journey through death symbolized by night – their grief, his and his mother's, at this final separation –

Second, the return from Keros – a resurrection, he is set free – he returns to a hero's welcome – he brings with him spring and a new song –

> *Why don't you*
> *get up old dead man*
> *well well well*
> *help me carry my row*
> *help me carry my row* [55]

Like the blues?

From one verse to the next, events may have little relationship to one another. The power comes in suggestion and compression.

Samuel Charters, *The Poetry of the Blues* (New York: Oak, 1963), 40, quoted in Rothenberg, ed., *Technicians of the Sacred*, 500.

If language was only heard, and not read, how much more did they hear in the stone?

In the language of archaeology, *fragments* are *reconstituted.*

Unprovenenced objects lack *contextual meaning.*

But removing the broken figurines from Keros, and attempting to reconstruct them, removes them from the context of place and ritual, the place of their meaning. In a world before writing, meaning was practised, not fixed. It was something renewed and reaffirmed through repetition. An object this immersed in place: can it hold any meaning outside of place? The archaeometrist's work, tying this figurine to that vein of marble: is this not a tacit recognition that meaning is inseparable from place?

Our approach to the meaning of the broken figurines must start with the journey to Keros –

>the danger of the crossing

>the sound of the wind, and of the sea breaking on rocks

>the release as the craft beaches

>the fear and fascination with the dark mouth of the cave

>Something given in gift
>must be drunk fully.

>Either we enter one system thoroughly
>or not at all.

Develop Biblical analogies – ?

Develop the search for Grave 28 into a symbolic quest for knowledge of death, which is forbidden knowledge – ?

We are kin to these bones
and to the hands that held them

they threw nets in the air

        arrested birds in flight

they carried songs back from the hunt

they dragged up fish into the day

    and dead, went

        curled into the ground

song birds come to us from there
children come to us from there
ancestors call to us from there
they wait for us (in there)
they wait for us

A single day as metaphor – ?

Begin before dawn.

Then a long procession from darkness to light, and to darkness again.

> Cyclical journeys?
>
> Out from home, and return, the protagonist's trip to the Cyclades mirroring the journey of an Early Bronze Age man to Keros.
>
> The protagonist's journey also internal, back through memory and time, to embrace and release Mother – and so be reborn?
>
> These in turn mirroring the journey of the human species – to the brink of extinction, then a return to "home" in Nature.

        barriers will crumble

        sea will sweep up the valley

        fields will be poisoned with salt

if we could go back to beginning –

erase everything that has happened since –

        knowledge, theory
        radio-carbon dating

erase, and begin again –

black stone against white stone

        – a full release from syntax

I give you a story.

                [audience:] *I give you another.*

I came and I saw.

                [audience:] *See so that we may see.*[56]

A man walks in circles on a bare stage, concentric circles, getting smaller all the time. He is naked, almost, and it is dark, almost. This is the storm at sea, and he is lost and going down.[57]

        death alone endures

        death unites us with the ancestors

One day a man picked up a stone from the beach
and it slipped into his hand like the waist of a woman.

I want a book of simple sentences.

The kind you run your finger down.

A book about a time when the book was inconceivable

when the idea of fixing language to surface
holding still the ripple moving outward from the mouth

                – inconceivable

who would have dared stop the fish dance
that set the children squealing?

He came upon a book about the Haida, a nation living on the islands called Haida Gwaii off the northwest coast of Turtle Island. Though devastated, like all indigenous cultures, by the arrival and occupation of European colonizers and Christian missionaries, the Haida, in part due to their geographical isolation, managed to hold on to their culture and their traditions better than most of the other First Nations of the Americas. Nevertheless, 90 per cent of the population of Haida Gwaii died in the 19th century, mainly from smallpox and other diseases brought to the islands by the Europeans.

The Haida were an oral culture until the missionaries arrived and wrote down the Haida language, the better to proselytize and colonize. By the end of the 19th century, the missionaries had translated parts of the Bible into Haida and attempted to codify a Haida grammar.

In 1900, a young American linguist and ethnographer named John Swanton travelled to Haida Gwaii and stayed for a year. Unlike other scholars of the day who were content to paraphrase the stories of the oral cultures they studied, Swanton, assisted by a bilingual Haida man known by his Christian name Henry Moody, transcribed, word for word, the epic stories and myths told to him by master Haida poets still living at the time.[58]

Eighty years later, a Canadian poet and scholar named Robert Bringhurst began studying the Haida language and Swanton and Moody's transcriptions. At the turn of the millennium, Bringhurst published his translations of the master Haida poets and myth-tellers, together with his reflections on the nature of oral poetry and myth.[59]

pick up shells
pick up stone

pick up bone

they cut sharply to the centre of something[60]

Reading comes before writing, Bringhurst says.[61]
Reading is as primitive as it gets.

We read animal tracks, scat, the set of ears.
We read the flight of birds and the surface of the sea.

We read leaves, teeth, facial expressions,
the clearing of a throat.

      a goat's udder so full
      it brushed the earth

Bringhurst writes that, in Native cultures, the gods are "innumerable, numinous, mortal, and local."[62]

How do I conceive of a world in which the gods are innumerable? A world in which everything surrounding me has a voice?

If I cannot conceive of such a world, how can I read the figurines?

    Marry an animal.

    Teach a story, one line at a time.

    Walk in darkness in memory of them.

(lawn mowers, weed whackers, car alarms –
the loneliness is everywhere)

I remember a room I passed, an open door. It was quiet inside but for intakes of breath, eruptions of mirth, chests patted in exclamation.

Words were being carved out of air.

the shoreline gone, the cliff collapsed –
villages fall through space onto the rocks below

> *Lost*
> *Pulled from the oar*
> *Pulled under –*
>
> *But on the beach that spring*
> *He appeared –*
> *Sure in my hand*

Bringhurst: *A myth is story, and it is a story that insistently recurs: a piece of timelessness caught like an eddy in narrative time. Once the story is known, a single image or even a single word can evoke it.*[63]

Could the figurines be just that – a single image from the most important story of the culture?

Not the representation of a god, but a freeze-frame in a story that everyone knew?

As Bringhurst observed[64] of the great Haida poets, perhaps the same could be said of the Cycladic carvers: they inherited a material (marble) and tools (emery, obsidian, pumice). And they inherited an image that was central to the people's story. The carver remade the image, as a poet recites an epic. And each carver gave the image something of himself, as each poet does the story.

of the words they sang —
they opened their mouths and they were there

    perched

    taking wing

Texts For The End of Time?

What Keros is made of:

Its fifteen square kilometres of mountainous, precipitous, and mostly arid land rise to 432 metres above sea level at the centre of the island, which is largely composed of marble; more specifically, white fine-grained marble dominates over coarse-grained, grey-white, and grey dolomite marble, the former forming mostly solid masses with many fractures. There are also thin layers of reddish yellow marble along the south coast. The marble alternates with schist in places, such as in the east of Keros and on the islet of Gourgari, off the bay of Tiliaos on the north-east coast, along a zone extending from the small bay of Phiro on the south coast of the island to the site of Koanakia on the north coast and to the west, opposite the islet of Daskalio. A thin layer of granite, rich in quartz, penetrates the schist range of the west coast, and small quantities of magnetite occur inside the marble mass at Tsigris, in the eastern part of the island.[65]

as refugees do, we wait
　　　and tell each other the stories of our lives –

Sea took them –
Swallowed bones

The monuments of the dead outnumber the monuments of the living.[66]

Bringhurst makes the point that oral literature, story-telling, begins and ends with formulaic phrases. This is universal, he says, and not restricted to what we call aboriginal cultures.[67] "Once upon a time." "Happily ever after." We grow up with these phrases, delight in them as children. They signal to us: listen!

Sea gave me child

What words did the Early Bronze Age storytellers use to begin the story of the woman in the stone? What words did they use to invoke spring?

Invent formulaic phrases?

Invent invocations?

---

darkness is another kind of death –

> *that night*
> *the moon died*

Four lines, an essence. I see them in front of me. I repeat them over and over. I tell myself I should turn on the light and write them down, but sleep is delicious. I am heavy with it, immobilized. I know I am fooling myself, but I am sure that this time, in the morning, I will remember.

Leave the process bare, exposed – ?

John Berger says somewhere that process is the true subject of contemporary art.

John Berger, *Selected Essays*, ed. Geoff Dyer (New York: Vintage, 2001).

The nose is the predominant feature on the faces of the figurines. But look at a human skull: viewed from the side, the face is almost a flat plane, tilted back at the top. The nasal bone is small and fragile and easily broken off. The flesh of the nasal bone is no more enduring than the flesh of the body. And yet it is that one feature of the face that is given permanence in the figurines.

I remember a self-portrait I drew, as a young man:

>an elongated, featureless face
>a prominent, elongated nose

Paint gave the faces identity. Now there is only a blank mask.

The Early Bronze Age people must have known that pigments were impermanent, that only the form would endure.

>– Nothing happened.

>– Nothing?

>– I held them in my hand, and nothing happened.

Elaborate the protagonist's character?

In him, embody fear and longing?

Bring in a refugee, with an urgent story to tell?

Into the mix of voices, one new voice arrives.

Reaching some conclusion is essential.

If there is not something left behind, then this has been for nothing.

swim fast fish!
bring morning back to us!

Something that's equal to them. That's the closest I can come to a statement of intent. I listen to the Bach cello suites and think, like that. But what would be the equivalent in words? Poetry, of course, but of a special order. *The Duino Elegies? The Four Quartets?* Something that goes beyond particulars of place and time, penetrates to something to which we can only allude. Most of the time I don't listen to music. It's silence I prefer now. I'm listening for something. I don't know what it is. Something to be given to me, that's one way of saying it. But I know it never will.

how to live: how to face death —
that is the one question we are left with

For all that we know — the data, the lists, the precise analysis of crystal and grain — for all that we know, we understand nothing. All that precision of language has brought us no closer to answering the question: what does this form mean, that I hold in my hand and that warms to my touch? What can it tell us?

> There is the body before it carries the child
> and there is the body after it brings us the child
> and there is the body going away from us, towards death.
>
> And there is death.
>
> And there is the body cleansed in the grave or the fire.

In aboriginal cultures, Bringhurst tells us, a dominant creature, one at the top of the food chain, carries the deceased to the next world. In Haida Gwaii, it was the orca whale.[68] In the Cyclades, what fish or animal bore this responsibility? Or was it a boat, decorated with images of animal spirits, sailed by the tribe's best hunter?

As the Haida's world was invaded and their culture assaulted by Christians — totem and mortuary poles cut down, houses levelled, ceremonies banned, forests ruthlessly logged — as the Haida, in one person's lifetime saw their world changed beyond belief, so perhaps did the Early Bronze Age inhabitants of the Cyclades experience a cataclysm that was beyond anything their story could explain. Invaders? An epidemic? A volcanic eruption? Imagine: if the cave on Keros collapsed and suddenly their access to the underworld was blocked, their only way of sending down the dead. A cataclysm literally beyond belief. Who would ensure fertility, the return of spring? Who would implore the gods to remember them? Could this have been the defining event that led to the "death" of Early Cycladic culture?

Of course, this is nothing more than speculation....[69]

There were raptors, no doubt – but just as the islands were small, perhaps it was the songbirds that carried the souls of the dead to Keros, flitting in swarms, singing together on their fall migration – and it was the duty of the son to carry the bones of his mother after them.

There was a time when I could recall the sequence of my summers in perfect order – the summer of that holiday, the summer of that job or furnished room. And then the sequence became too long, and my youth blurred, and the narrative line of my life faltered. And now, my younger years are distant – they have become my myth-time.

This journey, to penetrate the myth-time and leavings of a people who lived 4,000 years ago – is it really any different from looking back into the haze of my own beginnings?

My mother remembers the moment of my birth.

Bringhurst on classical Haida sculpture – but this seems just as true of the figurines and the copies of them sold in museum gift shops:

There is always an idea, envisioned in the substance by the artist, and clinging to the substance, yet perfectly able to leave the substance behind.... A molded plastic copy of a piece of Haida art is nevertheless always a disappointment, because the form has lost its bite. Paraphrases of classical Haida literature fail on precisely the same ground. The form must be reborn when it moves to a new substance; this occurs not when it is copied, but when it is reenvisioned and recarved.[70]

    They explained the figurines by making another.

    Carving another kept the story alive.

Without the books of the Bible, what would a future civilization make of a crucifix found in a grave? How would a future archaeologist reconstruct the life story of Jesus, and the meaning attached to it, from that single, unadorned object? Two bare, crossed lines of unequal length is a symbol potent enough to give meaning to the world, but only for those who know the story.

The Cycladic figurines are no different: a symbol, a single image isolated from a long story. And because this image was regenerated endlessly throughout the life of a culture, and made of a material that required skill and time to work, can we not at least assume that it was the central story of the culture? But there is no book to turn to. The story, the entire cosmology that surrounded it, is lost to us. We are left with a single frame from an epic narrative, from a time when humans had but a small place in the world. And so it becomes important to imagine the world that surrounded them, the plants and animals. But even that is lost to us – the forests cut down, the topsoil washed away, the wild animals slaughtered to extinction. Only, perhaps, the migration of the songbirds is a kind of memory. Their story, at least, is still there, written in the sky – though men slaughter them with buckshot for sport.

    all things have names –

    were the figurines named as a single entity, or individually?

Giacometti sketched the figurines in 1937, from photographs of them reproduced in *Cahiers d'Art*. He sketched works of art throughout his life, everything from prehistoric to contemporary art. Many of his sketches were made from photographs. His three sketches of Cycladic figurines are in pen and ink, on a single sheet of paper.[71]

Two figurines are side-by-side, headless – perhaps it is the same figurine. Giacometti seems to have been focussed on the torso and the external contours, over-scoring heavily the contour lines. There are horizontal creases across the abdomen, and a vaginal cleft. But the legs are not accurately reproduced. The sketch is perhaps unfinished.

At the bottom of the page is another figurine, laboriously shaded, as is the shadow it casts. But the sketch looks unlike a figurine, except for the crossed arms. The torso is strangely thick, and there is a kind of flat cloth covering the genitals.

These do not help, either.

The ossuary at Verdun, on the First World War battlefield, contains the bones of 300,000 French soldiers whose bodies were so mutilated by exploding shells, rats, and decomposition that they were unidentifiable.[72]

He is obsessed with graves.

What they put in them. What they take out.

> *Stone endures,* he writes.

> *But even stone does not endure forever.*

Another poor sleep. Woken several times in the night by blustering winds. At first light, the dogs start; at six, the bells. Sunday morning. Cumuli hurtling out of the north.

I put on my parka and head off to meet Daphne in front of the supermarket. I love these walks down into town from my room high above. This walk takes me through the children's playground (I never see children playing) and along an old country road that is being engulfed by the spreading town. The last remaining open field is littered with garbage. Tall bamboo forms a windbreak on two sides. It sways and clatters in the wind. That's all I hear until I pass, and then it's wind and songbirds, and more church bells. When I get to the supermarket, it's traffic. I sit on a low wall and wait. Trucks with men wearing camouflage pull in at the cafe next door.

Daphne arrives in a small red Peugeot, a white cotton sunhat pulled low over her eyes. Daphne Lalayannis: conservator at the Naxos archaeological museum. I told her I'm looking for Early Cycladic cemeteries and she offered to help. I told her I want to find Phyrroges but failing that we could look for another cemetery I've read about called Louros Athalasou. They're supposed to be in the same area, in the south-west part of the island. Daphne pulls out a museum booklet with a map showing the location of archaeological sites on the island, but the map is not to scale and the locations are only approximate. The topo map I've brought indicates cemeteries, but not prehistoric ones. Daphne has never come across one on her country rambles. I'm beginning to think this could turn into a wild goose chase, but the sky is clearing, promising a sunny day for a hike. We decide to go anyway. In my shirt pocket is the photograph of the figurine from Grave 28.

We head south on the coast road. The beaches are long and of white sand. In summer this is holiday heaven; in November it's desolate and forlorn, the sea whipped to white caps. I remark how many farm buildings there are in the lowlands we're driving through. Daphne corrects me: those are tourist accommodations: studios and villas and rooms. Families have abandoned their farms and built in pursuit of quick profit. There seems to be no planning, no centre. Dirt tracks veer off at all angles towards the buildings and the beach. Hand-lettered signs are stuck up here and there: Studios to rent. Taverna. Rooms. But everything is shuttered up.

A few kilometres farther on we pull off the road beside a taverna that appears to be open. Daphne goes inside to ask if anyone knows where the cemeteries are. A large black dog ambles over to the car and stares blankly at me. It's wearing a rope harness and has a tin bell hanging under it's neck. It looks harmless enough. I decide to get out. The dog shrinks aside, expecting a blow. The taverna is as forlorn as the beach. Chairs are stacked and roped in a corner of the terrace, the big outdoor grill is wrapped in plastic. I walk inside just as Daphne is saying goodbye. "Find the locals," seems to be the extent of the owner's help. They're newcomers, too.

We turn around and drive back a few hundred metres to a dirt road we saw leading inland. It's too rough for Daphne's car, so we leave it there and start walking. Off to the left is a low hillside with a small white church on it. That we can find on the topo. Now we know where we are, though we haven't a clue where we're going. But it seems as good a place as any to go inland. There's a machine on the hillside, too, near the church, with a jackhammer on the end of a long articulated arm. It batters away at the ground, sounding like a machine gun in slow motion. The noise follows us all day.

The road meanders between waist-high stone walls. On one side the wall is topped with a layer of concrete; on the other, with sun-bleached branches held down by stones. Daphne is a keen gardener and naturalist, and identifies the vegetation for me as we walk. Mediterranean oak. Two varieties of wild crocus. A native cedar so rare that cutting it is prohibited. A tree with a pale red berry; she can't remember the English name. The trees are small and stunted by the wind.

We are approaching a farm. Outside the gate, three bulls rest on the ground, chewing cud, each tethered to its own stake. Nearby, sheep and goats are milling in a pen. Two cats watch us from the top of a wall. An old woman with deeply furrowed skin comes out through the farmyard gate to greet us. She is wearing a faded dress, a scarf tied over her head, and sandals on her bare feet. I say a greeting in Greek, then step back and let the women confer. I hear the word Athalasou. The old woman points inland. Suddenly, we're moving, the old woman leading the way in through the gate. Daphne quickly explains: we're in the Athalasou valley. The woman says there are graves up there. She's not sure where, she's never seen them, she's never heard of a place called Phyrroges. She's taking us to a river that we can follow inland.

The woman leads us through her farmyard. The animals stare. We follow her up some steps and over a stone wall, then along a footpath that skirts a tilled field. We're walking single file. We turn right at the corner of the field, squeeze through a gate, duck under low branches, and stop on a patch of open ground. Sweeping past in front of us is a bone-dry river the width of a country road.

This is as far as the old women will go. She points and says there's a hamlet upstream and people there can help us find the graves.

We scramble down into the riverbed. It's fine white sand. Round stones the size of fists are lying loosely all over the place, making the footing tricky, but at least it's warmer down here: the trees and bushes on the banks are cutting the wind. A laurel bush is in bloom midstream. The valley is broad and flanked with hills and seems to curve in a long crescent towards the mountains that form the island's spine. Dominating them is Mount Zas, elevation 1,003 metres, highest mountain in the Cyclades and, in Greek mythology, the birthplace of Zeus.

The river meanders. We can never see far ahead. The banks rise and fall. Sometimes we're shoulder deep below ground level. Sediment is piled up in some places, swept away in others. There are mini-islands of heaped up rocks and sand and branches; some have vegetation growing on them. Stretches of pure sand alternate with stretches of loose stones. At one point the banks dip low on both sides and tire tracks lead down and across the riverbed. The land looks good for agriculture. This must be floodplain soil. We pass a field of potatoes irrigated with black pipes lying on the ground. We pass another field being worked by a farmer on a tractor. He doesn't see us, we walk on. It's slow going in the sand and shifting stones, so we clamber up onto the bank and try following tire tracks that run alongside the river. But the ground is uncultivated and covered in wild thyme. It's dry and spiky and painful to the ankles, so we slide back into the riverbed and carry on.

Suddenly, round a bend: an outcrop of marble thrusting up through the river bank. I'm enraptured by the cream-coloured rock, the crystals glinting. The bank is high here. It's been undercut by the current. The marble protrudes in slabs a few inches thick and a few feet wide, tilting upwards at a slight angle. Pieces have broken away. Some lie loose on the slab below, others have fallen onto the riverbed. I pick up a small piece and snap it open: fine-grain marble, small crystals, with some imperfections giving it a slight pinkish tint. I pick up another piece, the size of a half-pound of butter. It's smooth and shaped by the river's abrasion. It stands upright, unsupported on my open palm. The front and back are flat, the sides slightly flared. There's a curving protrusion one could imagine to be a shoulder. Holding the marble, it's not hard to understand why the Early Cycladic carvers sometimes worked with the shape that was given to them, making schematic figurines. And yet it was always a human form that they saw in the stone, not a fish or a bird or a goat. And not just the human form, but the female form, over and over. I slip the marble into my pocket and we walk on.

There is more laurel in bloom. A cactus has taken root on a sandbar. We find the skull of a goat. Around every bend we find more and more human refuse: plastic water bottles, plastic shopping bags snagged on branches, tin cans, sacks that once held fertilizer or chemicals. Underfoot: empty shotgun shells, the plastic casings bright red.

It's after noon. Church must be out. We can hear more and more blasts from guns. The shots are getting louder as we move inland. The hunters are shooting migrating songbirds. Occasionally we hear birdsong, when there's a lull in the wind, but it's the noise of the booming guns that dominates. It's nerve-wracking. I can't tell which way the hunters are firing, and I don't know whether they can see us in the riverbed. I hope they are sporting hunters, shooting birds on the wing and not blasting waist-level into the bushes.

Another bend, another outcrop of marble. Here the slabs are three to five inches thick, just right for a figurine or a shallow marble bowl. A pink sweater is snagged on a bush. More flowers. More shotgun shells. More plastic. Then the riverbed widens and the banks dip low again. We are approaching another crossing. This one is well-used. Tire tracks are braided across a wide area. Suddenly – bells, a gamelan of bells. A flock of sheep and goats pours over the riverbank, a dusty Toyota pickup truck bumps along in their midst. The windows are open, two men inside are hooting and whistling. The animals are bleating and bumping into each other. When they get down into the riverbed they surge forward and spread out. The udders of the females are full and swaying. We wave. The truck stops midstream. The animals head for the foliage overhanging the far bank. The men get out and shout and wave their arms. They seem to be encouraging the flock to forage here. I venture another greeting, then step aside again and let Daphne and the younger of the two men talk. Neither man seems to be in a hurry, though I can see more and more of their flock disappearing upstream. The older man wears a baseball cap tied onto his head with a scarf knotted under his chin. He smiles at me and says a few words in Greek. I smile back and gesture that I don't understand. He smiles again and shrugs. We keep smiling. I hear the word Athalasou. The younger man is pointing and Daphne is nodding. Then it's goodbyes. The men shout and whistle, get back in their truck, and inch forward again. The sheep and goats jog back from all directions and flock around them. A few stragglers are reluctant to tear themselves away from the vegetation, but soon fall into place.

Daphne summarizes the intelligence. We're definitely in the Athalasou valley. The men have a farm nearby. An artesian well provides water for their animals and crops. There are graves nearby, too, on the hill above the valley. I peer along the length of her arm. "See that large tree, in the open? The one that's bigger than the others? Just below it, see that darker area? They say that's Louros Athalasou. They say we can see graves there. They say archaeologists dug there, but most of the graves were robbed by the local people first." What about Phyrroges? "They say it's over that way" she points to a ripple of low hills. "But they don't know where exactly. They've never seen it."

We are revitalized. We can see our destination. It's not the one I hoped for, but with sunset before six and no clear directions to Phyrroges, we set off for Louros Athalasou. It would be an easy few minutes walk except for the maze of stone walls. The farmer said to follow the road back where they came from, and turn in at the first house. The road leads out of the valley and around the flank of the hill. We try to keep the cemetery in sight, but the perspective changes as we walk. We find no farmyard or house, only a makeshift gate with a stone hut on the other side. It's empty, caked with animal shit. If we go any further up the road we'll lose sight of the cemetery. We decide to start uphill here.

The gate is heavy, made of rusty wire mesh tied to stakes in the ground. It's a struggle to pull it closed behind us. We cross the first field and look for a gate or step over the first stone wall. There's nothing. We climb over a low point in the wall and find ourselves in another field, also walled. We're like animals trapped in an enclosure, craning our necks, looking for a way out. I lead the way uphill, through thistle and thyme and rough ground, and find another place to scramble over. Daphne is shorter than I and has more difficulty. In the third field I notice sherds of pottery on the ground, fragments of clay pots and bowls the colour of the earth. They're mixed in with the pebbles and stones. Daphne says it's not unusual to find sherds in the countryside. She says they are often found scattered in a wide radius around the sites of old settlements. She doesn't know how old these ones are, or what they might indicate. I wonder silently whether they were discarded by the locals who looted the cemetery above us. I stoop and pick up a sherd, the lip of a bowl, and wonder aloud about keeping it. Daphne politely reminds me of the law of the land: leave things where you find them: who knows what information they may convey to an archaeologist exploring this area in the future.

We continue weaving back and forth, looking for low points in the walls to climb over. We can see the cemetery now, not far above us, but there is still another wall to get over. The zigzagging brings another discovery. Daphne spots it first: a circle of stones in the ground, a threshing circle. "They are not rare. Not old. They are everywhere. And what a perfect place for it, on the shoulder of this hill. There's a steady wind to blow the chaff away. Think of the women working here, the valley spread out below." I look at the stones. Some are slabs of schist. The grave are just above us. Were these taken from the grave structures and carried here to make the circle?

The last wall is the hardest. It's in bad repair, crumbling and overgrown with vegetation, making it impossible to see the ground on the other side. A recipe for a twisted ankle. We lower ourselves over carefully, and scramble up into the clearing.

This is what we find: Opened graves, at first barely discernible, holes half-filled with dirt. Low bushes and thistle conceal some of them. Schist slabs have been pulled aside: some are standing upright in piles of dirt, some have scratch marks on them, from steel tools. The ground is strewn with pebbles, rocks, chunks of marble. Patches of pink cyclamen are in bloom. Animal dung is everywhere. The defilement is unsettling. I think of old photographs: a field after battle, shell-holes and debris.

I pace it out: the cemetery is 30 paces wide and 120 paces long. My topo map tells me we are 50 to 60 metres above sea level, on the south side of the valley. We're facing north into the wind. The wind would have blown the stench of decomposition away from the settlement, if it was below us in the valley, or across from us on the south-facing hillside. This is a beautiful place to lie, with views to the high mountains inland and to the sea. One side of the burial ground is bordered by a low cliff, a long outcrop of marble. Pieces have fallen onto the ground. The large tree at the top is a cedar. When bodies were interred here, all this might have been forest.

There's so much that's never said. Mysteries I do not understand. Secrets, perhaps. Once my mother said to me, "There are things your father will never tell you. Things that happened." He calls me to him from a distance. "Let's talk!" But when I get there, he says nothing of the past.
    – Is there something you wanted to tell me?
    – Nothing.

He denies luring me with the promise of confidences, of things said at last. "Is a father not allowed to see his son?"

My mother sits beside me, restless to talk, but she skips and turns, never alighting for long on things that lie between us. She tells me she is not afraid of death, only the pain of dying. She tells me she will be with her mother and father, and her brothers – all gone before her. "As my life closes in, I have such a longing for family." But it's what's missing that I long for. And that torments me with the fear of losing it forever.

These folds that rise no further, and having risen, rest, and are embraced. Worm and leaf lay down upon them, and the flowers and the fragrant wild herbs took root upon them.

Where the land slips, or run-off scours the bank, where animal hooves wear paths on the hills and rivulets run down to the sea – there the folds come free and give us white.

These words that rise no further –

we turned where the river turned

Repetition is essential. Song, music, chants – this is repetition through short spans of time, in forms that unfold in time.

But what of forms that do not unfold in time? What would repetition be, other than an accumulation of identical, or near-identical, images – or variations on them, like variations in music?

What is the impact – and the implicit message – in making the same form again and again?

And what of the variations – are they evidence of individuality, pressing on the walls of tradition?

What of the rare "non-canonical" figurines – the seated figures, the musicians, the male hunters? Prized now for their remarkable plasticity and craft, their three-dimensionality – were these heretical acts of rebellion against the demands of society for endless repetition of the female with the folded arms? What was the penalty these rebels faced – ostracism? exile? death? Or were their carvings valued? Were these non-canonical figurines the secular art of their times?

Bringhurst: The power of a myth is in the way an individual tells it, not in the generic myth itself. To paraphrase a myth is to silence it.[73]

In the same way, the reproductions of the Cycladic figurines sold in museum gift shops are deceptions.

True, they are not passed off as real, like fakes sold on the art market. But the result is the same: they give space in the world to paraphrases. They silence the story.

In Haida mythology, men turn into spirits by walking through fire.
The spirit-beings sail around and between the islands, distant and ghost-like.
They circumnavigate in all weathers and seasons.
They approach shore only when bidden by shamans.
They cannot be seen, or their voices heard, except by shamans.
They are drawn to fire.
They attract and embrace women.[74]

Might not other island cultures view their surroundings in similar ways – the spirit-beings sailing around and between the islands, moving through all weathers and seasons, drawn to the warmth of fires and women? Was it spirits like these that called the bones of the dead to Keros, and called the image of all women, the figurines, to come, too?

Other species have songs.

In a world sparsely populated by humans, what dominated the acoustic landscape?

>   birds louder than hamlets

The telling of a myth can be a form of meditation. – Bringhurst.[75]

So, too, the making of a myth-time image.

Something spoke through them, geologic time, uncounted time. The great push upward of time.

>   and dung and leaf made soil

Does it matter that I walked on the same ground, crossed the same straits?
What I saw was not what they saw.
Gone are the forests and the wild animals.
Gone is *how* they saw.

Only the trajectory of the sun remains the same
but not the way sunlight reflects on the land –
forested then – now bare.

The wind and waves are perhaps the same
but currents may have shifted over 4,000 years.

Shoreline and horizon have surely changed –
plates collided – islands split in two.

Cliffs have fallen.
Streams have changed course.

But that outcrop of marble, protruding from the river bank
the piece that stood on my palm
already shaped by the abrading waters
already imbued with
something –

        with wonder
        with a surge of wonder and light

When we look at a figurine, the shadow of a people walks silently behind us.

Imagine the final decades, the final years. The population decimated or dispersed by some cataclysm. Imagine the last myth-tellers dying, drowning, speared in battle, killed by a blow to the skull. Or imagine them surviving, but with no one to listen to their recitation, the people dispersed in panic or despair, the language dying as the population thinned and mixed with other peoples. And one day there are only two myth tellers left, growing old, forgetting the stories they carried, or, if remembering them, with no one to teach them to. And then there is one. Of necessity, he learns the language of the people that surround him, wherever he has come ashore, or the language of those who have come ashore on his island. Refugee or survivor, perhaps slave, he sings the old songs at night or at dawn or while calling to the fish from shore. But no one understands what he is saying, he is an old man talking to himself, he is ignored. The stories crumble in his memory, and one day they are gone, and his body is buried or slipped into the sea.

Bringhurst: *Blind myth tellers ... are frequent in the record of oral poetry around the world.*[76] Blindness limits your usefulness in a hunter-gather society. Poetry was a way to contribute.

Is it possible that the carvers of the figurines were blind?
And sang, while working the stone?

As labour begets song.
As hunters sing to the spirits of animals.

I narrate the story of a contemporary man's voyage through the Cyclades, ending on Keros – ?

Follow this with the voice of an Early Bronze Age man taking the bones of his mother to Keros, and the voices of shamans and spirit-beings at sea.

But who will tell my story – ?

Or, a narrator describes my journey, while I speak in the first person and other voices intrude, including the Early Bronze Age man on his

---

voyage to Keros. But how far back can this regress? Who is this narrator, and what is *his* story – ?

And so history is born – the prose mind, seeking explanation, causal linkages, reaching back further and further, wanting origin.

Everything spoke —

        wind

                bird

                      tree

sea

    fish

They studied earth: it revealed seed.
They studied tree: it revealed fire.
They studied stone: it revealed woman.

Transcript: Olga Philaniotou, archaeologist.[77]

How do you feel about excavating graves? In other countries, the aboriginal peoples are still alive to object to the desecration of their ancestral burial grounds. But here in Greece, there are no known descendants of the Early Cycladic people.

Sometimes I ask myself whether we have the right to do it. But how else would we know about the Early Bronze Age if we had not excavated the graves? I feel I do have the right – the fact that I have this skill and I can communicate this knowledge and make it available to other people. One has to find out about history.

I sit alone for hours in the museum.
I am like the faithful, kneeling.

Is it only the mad who hear?
Is it my insistence that renders them silent?

What I held in my hand – was it a god or a poem ?

Not the horror of the blown-open body
but the sudden stillness –
the sudden unexpected *at rest*.

To see inside that – and beyond –

But what do I know of gods?
I have only the weight of stone
that my hand remembers

    The nets pull up empty.

    Boys hook squid along the breakwater, but the blue fin tuna is gone.

    The old songs and prayers go unanswered.

    There is no time left.

What words did they sing to the figurines? What words did they use to speak of them? Were they the words of the common man, or the exalted words of the priest? Were the words already archaic, from a past that was as distant to them as they are to us? Perhaps the meaning they attached to the figurines was itself ancient. They had a prehistory, too. Their language, like ours, had distant roots. And just as Pound struck resonance by employing a syntax of the distant past, evoking meaning beneath meaning, so the language they used to address the figurines may have evoked times and peoples distant even to them, peoples of a greater knowledge and another way, still, of knowing.

>there is always past
>and a time before past
>
>(– and a stirring of memory)

And we, in the vulgar present, on the edge of ruin, at the end of time, prepare to slip under the waves, though we prepare not at all.

We announce a new sortie, call up the old gods in the service of our crimes, call for construction on the scorched fields, on the barren fields, above the empty and heaving sea.

They carried everything they needed on the tongue.

Giambattista Vico says there are three ages in a cycle of history (– this according to Northrop Frye): First, a mythical age, the age of gods. Then, a heroic age, the age of aristocracy. And finally, the age of the people – after which, Vico says, the cycle starts again. Each age, Vico says, has its own type of verbal expression. First, "the poetic"; then "the heroic or noble"; and finally "the vulgar." Each age is characterized by a different use of language – first, poetic, then allegorical, then descriptive.[78]

We, then, are people immersed in the descriptive, trying to make sense of the poetic.

In the mythical/poetic phase of language, all words are concrete, Frye says.
There are no verbal abstractions.
Ideas are anchored in the physical.
Subject and object are not clearly separated.
Emotion and intellect are not clearly separated.
Prose is discontinuous.

Words are a way to power, Frye says, a way of getting a handle on things.[79]
But we have only this silent image — and not even a name for it.
It is we who are powerless.

A conflict — a dichotomy — ?

My voice, narrating in prose, embedded in abstractions and descriptive language.

- versus -

The voices of the Early Bronze Age culture, embedded in a mythical, metaphorical view of the world, and direct experience of life's processes and cycles.

The lure of poetic language is the lure back, to a direct experience, and a direct expression of the experience.

My conflict: the struggle to release myself from the hold of prose, the grip of the intellect. Look at this notebook, this schemata of ideas, this searching for clues in books and abstractions.

I went about it all wrong, didn't I?

The distancing began with writing things down.

It's a large room at the top of a narrow staircase, with a high ceiling and windows along a far wall. Every available space is filled with artifacts in one stage or another of restoration and conservation. The wall opposite the door is covered floor to ceiling with wooden drawers in a metal frame. There are 10 columns of drawers, with 20 drawers in each column. Each column is labelled at the top with a number, 1 to 10, from left to right, printed in black felt pen on yellow cards. Each drawer is labelled with its own yellow card. The drawers are the final resting place of artifacts that have been cleaned and catalogued.

On the wall to the right of the door are shelves holding restored pottery, each object labelled with a yellow card. Three long tables fill the rest of the room. They are laden with cardboard boxes full of artifacts. On the floor beneath the tables, and between the tables, and leaning against the walls, are more boxes and clear plastic bags. The bags are full of unwashed sherds, and a single yellow card inside. They strike me as jigsaw puzzles from hell. Imagine someone handing you a bag of perhaps a hundred jigsaw pieces covered in dirt and telling you they don't know how many puzzles are in the bag. They warn you that some pieces are almost certainly missing. You may end up with a single, incomplete puzzle, or several puzzles; you will probably have leftover pieces belonging to other puzzles in other bags, or still underground. After days of cleaning and examining the pieces, you may end up with no puzzle at all, nothing worth even partially reconstructing. This is your job. You are under pressure to assemble as many puzzles as you can, as quickly as possible. New bags are arriving all the time.

Daphne's work table is beside the door. It's a small table adjoining one of the long tables. On the long table beside her is work waiting to be done. Under a moveable lamp with a magnifying glass in the middle is a small, shattered vase, embedded in a clump of earth. She is removing the soil, cleaning each sherd, and reassembling the vase. On the table is a plastic syringe, which she uses to apply drops of various cleaning liquids. Nearby is a jar holding her tools – a toothbrush, dental picks, tweezers, more syringes. Also on the table is a sheet of paper, on which she documents every step she takes in the cleaning and restoration process, including the precise mixtures of the solvents and glues she uses. This becomes part of the documentation for each artifact. She says it's important to record what chemicals have been applied to the object in case someone wants to do a scientific analysis of the material later, or take apart an object that has been glued together.[80]

A room in the basement contains more artifacts, and more bags full of sherds.

Writing was invented for commercial transactions, the counting of sheep, maintaining records of trade and debts. Perhaps the Early Bronze Age people of the Cyclades did write, but their commercial records were seasonal, annual – there was no need to fix them in stone. If records were made in clay or on wood or leather, they have gone back into the earth.

> it is spring.
> something has to die.[81]

History is the stories told to us of people who are no longer here.

Stories told to the young are hazily remembered, replaced with other stories that mean more to them. It is only the stories that are repeated, incised in memory – it is only those stories that we can push against. As the oar pushes against the sea.

All the rest pass under us, hissing brine.

If, as Frye says (riffing on Vico) that human history begins with a mythical age, and that it was an age of gods (plural), and that the "central conception" unifying human thought and imagination during that age was of a "plurality of gods"[82] – if the gods were *plural*, then why was only one image made by the Early Cycladic people, and endlessly repeated?

No one knows! We must do more research! We must dig! [83]

And we, in this vulgar age of decline, flirting with old practices and many-headed goddesses, we are uncomprehending. We explain some things, speculate about others, but we do not penetrate to the centre of things. We do not live in the certainty that the soaring raptor is a god. Or the whale. Or the mountain. Some cataclysm would be needed to take us back there. I do not mean those of us who are here now, but our species, those of us who may survive.

Begin with description, because this is the age I am living in – ?

Allow the protagonist to express his own theories and opinions, and by this reveal his character – ?

I read everything several times now, my eyes loop back again and again. Words slip past unregistered, no longer making impressions. It's as if I'm slipping back through writing to that open space where words sounded once, and were taken by the wind.

If we kill, we must allow ourselves to be killed.

What does the wave say?

Art historians study individual artists or groups of artists in their social and cultural context. Where there are no written records, art historians look to archaeology for context. With the Cycladic figurines, the context remains largely unknown. As a result, art historical studies of the figurines have been mostly subjective and focussed on the aesthetic qualities and craftsmanship of individual figurines.

In the 1960s, an archaeologist named Pat Getz-Gentle[84] began taking an art historical approach to the study of the figurines. She looked for stylistic similarities among individual figurines in museums and collections all over the world. She studied the slope of the shoulders, the thickness of the arms, the placement of the breasts, the mathematical proportions of thighs to torso. She believed she saw indications of individual carving styles, and attributed specific figurines to individual carvers. She gave the carvers names, according to the museum or collection where the figurines she claimed to be their master works were found: The Naxos Sculptor, the Copenhagen Sculptor, the Goulandris Sculptor, and so on. She also claimed that these master sculptors consciously pre-planned their figurines according to proportional canons, and that it was possible to trace a stylistic development in their "careers."

Getz-Gentle's work, published by university presses and art museums in the USA, has met with criticism from archaeologists. Some regard her claim to be able to see stylistic developments in the "careers" of individual carvers as "speculative fictions."[85] The fundamental resistance to her conclusions is based on the fact that only a small minority of the figurines that she has attributed to individual sculptors have been proven to be genuine artifacts. Most are unprovenanced. A few have been found to be fakes.

Focussing on individual figurines, looking for marks of the individual, seems to me to be a rejection of what the figurines are "saying" by the fact of their repetition and regeneration through centuries: that the repeated form is what matters, not the individual expression of it. Every figurine is unique, of that there is no doubt. Every one has a tick, an imperfection, an asymmetry. And clearly there is an evolution in style through the centuries: figurines made in 2700 BC collectively look different from those made three or four hundred years later. But the essential form remained unchanged – left arm above right, head tilted back, feet pointed down – until the culture collapsed and the form itself disappeared. Focussing on stylistic differences, looking for expressions of the individual, is a betrayal of the form. Perhaps it is a kind of blasphemy. Master carvers there probably were, but the meaning art historians give to *master* is very different from that of the spiritual mind.

What if we step back even further from the object as object, and consider the possibility that the importance of the figurines lay as much, or more, in the process of making them as in the finished object itself. And that the power inherent in the figurine comes not from the final shape of the stone, its beauty or symmetry, or even how closely it adheres to an idea of the form, but from its embodiment of a lengthy process involving the whole community, a process of training and devotion and attending that reached its culmination in the finishing touches of a master carver. Perhaps the meaning lay in what came before the finished object. If the act of making the figurine was a priestly act, a transcendent experience for the master carver, then the residue of that transcendence rested in the stone. Perhaps it is that residue, that aura, that we feel now in the presence of a real figurine, and which we don't feel in the presence of a gift shop reproduction. So, perhaps the value of a figurine to its "owner" was less its aesthetic qualities, or even its uniqueness, but in its residue of spiritual "charge" imbued in the stone by the carver. Perhaps the more enlightened the carver, the deeper his spiritual practice, the more cherished the figurine.

> who saw the sea's motion in the stone
> who cut slowly
> who studied the form so long it became part of him

I loop back and loop back. I am seeing words on a page, but I am not seeing them as I used to. I am seeing strings of words, but not what they signify. Meaning is not penetrating. Lines pass through my field of vision, but nothing holds. Words have become marks on a surface.

We must know them first as the hands that made them knew them –
    as weight
    as heft and balance
    as texture and smell
    as crystals sticking to fingertips
    as dust

Glass keeps us out –
              keeps us too much in our ideas about things

My mother's health is stable, but the charge is wearing down. I feel suspended in time, but I am mistaken – my own charge is running down just as quickly. I am focussed on her time left, measuring my steps by hers. She binds me to her, by fine threads of need.

I could break free, and away, but the tearing –

> *I am the woman of the rock.*
> *(I am the woman of the rock.)*
>
> *I am the bones of the land.*
> *(I am the bones of the land – look!)*
>
> *I am the gift of the sea.*

Death happens once, in all its intensity, and cannot happen again.

Open and close the book with narrated episodes – ?

A bookend structure, in which the descriptive encases the metaphorical, and the third person the first – ?

If I could strip away everything, forget time and the weight of language, maybe then I could reach it – the knowledge contained in the form.

>
> as reaching through leaves for an apple
>
> as fingering the loam for tubers
>
> Imagine – white linen gloves given to us
> when we enter a sculpture gallery
>
> > ball turning in socket
> > clavicle lifting
> > joint reading angle
>
> – by this, memory enters the bone

Catalogues say nothing of what the hand knows.
Dimensions are given, but not weight.

How they appear to the eye is minutely described
but not how they lay in the palm –

The broad upper torso is trapezoidal, with markedly inclined angular shoulders ...

[cross-fade]

The legs are joined, differentiated by a cleft that is wide and deep at the front, shallower at the back ...

[cross-fade]

A shallow incision at the lower end of the rather flat belly and two diagonal converging lines at the groin mark the broad pubic triangle ...

[cross-fade]

The spine is not indicated. The shallow rear leg cleft differentiates the buttocks ...

[cross-fade]

The slightly arched foot stands on tiptoe ...

> *These are the bones of our dead.*
>
> – We do not find bones.
>
> *These are the bones of our dead. Look!*

Old break. Small old chip on the little toe ...

[cross-fade]

Surface eroded, with occasional incrustation ...

[cross-fade]

Front of the left foot missing. Recent chips on the front of the right foot ...

[cross-fade]

Old break. Old chip ...

[cross-fade]

Head and neck missing ...

[cross-fade]

Details difficult to discern.[86]

The old fear comes upon me.

When will it be announced?

The cemeteries do not lie.

I was first captivated by their disarming simplicity, their abstracted facelessness that suggested absolutes waiting to be named.

And by the whiteness of the stone. Like undressed skin. Like bone.

Later, when I learned they came from graves, it was death that drew me on.

> *song, rise up, they need you*
> *go to them*
> *tell them we speak of them*
> *tell them we wait for them*
>
> *smoke of our hearth, rise up*
> *go to them*
> *help them to lie still*
>
> *send animals to lie down with them*
> *send worm and ant to help them on their way*

He is obsessed with bones. He thinks only about bones, not flesh. He thinks one day he will try carving bones in marble. He will become a bone artist. He will be known as the bone artist. He will collect bones, too, the bones of wild animals picked up in forests, the jawbones of spawning salmon. He would like to study bones, too, the science of osteology. But it is too late for that.

> Opening the journals of a man obsessed by the figurines – ?
>
> The journals have been sealed in an archive.
>
> A researcher is given white gloves to handle them.
>
> The journals are fragmented and inconclusive.

another obsession: archiving
storing up history

compare this with letting go
consigning a body to a grave

        then, death had substance
        the stench of it rose out of the grave

        bones had to be moved
        stacked with older bones

        parents, sisters, uncles –

        room made in the grave
        for the next generation

        who could have imagined an end to it all?

That old photograph in the museum: the one looking down into an excavated grave. In the grave there is a skeleton, curled on its side, knees to its chest, hands in front of its face – but that may not be true. It may be the archaeologist lying in the grave, clothed and alive, demonstrating prehistoric burial practices, knees to his chest, hands to his lips, trying not to laugh while the photographer fiddles beneath a draped black hood and the workers light cigarettes, joking, standing outside the frame, one of them mimicking a priest giving rites. But I want a skeleton. That is how I want to remember it – a skeleton, uncovered, intact, as yet undisturbed. I see this because I want to see this. Because death is everywhere, and smoke is drifting on the horizon.

I remember our first conversation.

I said to her, music begins with the breath, with the body and the dance.

She argued for mathematics, serial techniques.

Descriptive language has always been there, used for haggling, constructing, managing. But it is only in Vito's third phase, the vulgar, that descriptive language becomes what Frye calls "culturally ascendant." That required the ascendancy of science, which is based on descriptions of what, ideally, we can experience with our senses. But we know now that much of what we see is an illusion. The sun doesn't rise. Physics is undoing the separation of observer and observed. Subject and object have become inseparable again, and language, Frye says, is reverting to the metaphorical.[87]

How do I construct a deified world?

The gods placed limits on our reach –
we have broken their hold.

We have dragged the oceans raw.

More and more he is drawn to the vitrine of fragments. Rows of legs laid out side by side – then torsos – then heads. He thinks of photographs he has seen of ossuaries, rows of dry bones neatly stacked, skulls stacked, femurs laid up like cordwood.

It was what the breaks revealed that drew me – the raw substance inside the form.

I thought of broken bones. I think of them still as broken bones.

Where is the fingertip drawn to now – the smooth contour or the raw edge?

Which cuts deeper, and more true?

Frye distinguishes magic from poetry this way: Magic acts upon the world. Poetry acts upon the listener. Magic's prescribed formulas cannot be varied by even a syllable. Poetry emancipates magical language.[88]

Seen in this light, the figurines belong to magic.

What dances did they dance in the night?
        – I don't see, I don't hear.

What dances?
        – I came alone.

What words filled the night?
        [silence]

What words?
        – Nothing followed me here.

What songs did they sing?

                                          [silence]

What songs?

                    deer bolts through the cut

                    owl flees the screeching steel

We must do everything we can – make deliberate effort – to subvert the mind that observes.

                speak of the sea as if it were listening

                    we build barriers against the sea

                speak of the trees as if they were listening

                    we crawl down into the earth

                    and drag out riches

The figurines are not seized moments. They point to something that is outside time. It is, perhaps, the something that all spiritual practices point to. The history of religious art is a history of pointing.

For all their differences, the figurines remain a single image. To speak of them in the plural ("they") leads us away from the singular. It is a trick of grammar. It turns them into objects. It is a deceit of our age. (There are many deceits of our age.) The figurines belong to an age prior to the separation of subject and object. We might get closer to their meaning – closer to their power – if we speak of them, not in the plural, but as "she" in the singular. Let's see if that leads us closer to the mind that says "crow," not "a crow."

She lifts us out of history.
She is beyond hunger and fear.

It's the grasping at things that drives them away.
(Fish scatter into deeper pools.)

I wanted epiphany.

I dream still of a resonant line of words.

Wanting not her, but all the earth.[89]

I am holding a stone picked up in a riverbed.

(It is a beginning.)

My hand encircles it.

This is how it was.

(There are many beginnings.)

> Narrator lays down markers – ?
>
>   "Now we are here."
>
>   "Now we are some time later."
>
>   "Now we will go back to an earlier time."

It doesn't matter anymore what names we give the colours of the sea –
steel blue, ultramarine, aquamarine –

    the crossing is almost over

Barques are frequently storm-bound down there, and wait for weeks for favourable winds.[90]

    death was at close quarters –

    fish suffocating
    birds brought down
    throats slit

    their fortresses
    had
    narrow entrances –

    death was an arm's reach away

Always small pieces. Small bundles of words.

> We inflict our rage upon the world.
> We have left too great a mark upon the world.
>
> Where have we not entered without knocking?
>
> Dogs howl under the stars.

> A chorus of my anger and grief?

> Her body warmed to mine.
>
> Her weight was personal.

this compulsion to explain —
never enough to see —

just see

sacred to the memory of

He opens another book.

After the last ice age, people all over Europe continued to hunt, fish, and gather wild foods. Some continued hunting and gathering for another 8,000 years. At the same time, people in Asia were learning to cultivate grains and pulses, to save seeds, and to domesticate animals for milk and meat. As early as 10,000 BC there were farming communities in the lands we now call Iran, Iraq, Syria, and Turkey. These agricultural societies developed for the next 3,000 years. Then, around 7,000 BC, at the beginning of what we call the Neolithic Period, people with agricultural skills began migrating north in large numbers. Some walked through Turkey and into Europe. Others moved from island to island across the Aegean Sea. They carried with them barley and flax and lentils, and they herded sheep and goats and cows and pigs. They brought with them, too, the idea of settled communities, permanent houses, cemeteries for the dead. The people of the Aegean Islands were the first in Europe to practice farming, though they continued to hunt and fish and gather wild foods, too. They were blessed with abundance. Once the migrants reached mainland Europe, they spread slowly across the continent in two great arcs: north, into eastern Europe, and west along the shores of the Mediterranean, then up river valleys into France and Spain. Because of a genetic mutation in the migrants, they became lactose-tolerant and could drink milk in large quantities. The resulting nutritional advantage gave them better survival rates and faster population growth, allowing them to slowly win out over the original hunter-gatherers of Europe. It took 3,000 years for agriculture to move across Europe, arriving last in the British Isles and Scandinavia.[91]

> Sea was always there, gnawing
> pulling down ramparts
> sweeping boats away to darkness
> breaking stone
>
> More sea than we could bear sometimes
> more death

our land rode high
anchored deep

We follow waters. We seek the source, the beginning of things.

He is moving from vitrine to vitrine, silently, slowly. He holds his hands behind his back. He is bent over, looking. He straightens and breathes and turns toward the window at the end of the room. He sees the vitrine that faces the window, the one with the seven figurines, upright in a line. The sunlight renders them in silhouette. They are seven darkened forms. He sees seven silhouettes of the female form, suspended in sunlight. And that is all.

Words. And even when words are not there, the pull of words.

What have we forgotten, by writing it down? What did we remember, before?

How to live in the world was not a "body of knowledge." There was no place outside of it, from where to consider it, as something apart.

It was not referenced.

> Competing tendencies – ?
>
> > deconstruct, or leave in pieces
> > - versus -
> > construct, or reassemble
>
> Is this better played out as an internal conflict of the protagonist, or as a conflict between the protagonist and someone else? (– but whom?)

We can be thankful for time's ravages, for the action of bacteria and worm. She is cleansed now, of pigment. She is pure form.

The eyes, hair, and adornments that were painted on her meant something to those who held her, but that meaning is lost to us. As it should be. Grief and ecstasy are private experiences, particular to time and place.

After the dissolution of the body, the living are left with memory (fading) and abstractions (growing).

Until, in time, what is left is a naked figurine.

Consider the enigmatic drooping feet. Others have seen them as an indication of how the figurines were positioned – leaning against a wall, or lying down in imitation of sleep or death. But perhaps they are simply an affirmation of the way the marble came into the world, as thin slabs. Naturalistic feet extending forward from the body would have required thicker pieces of marble. What we can explain this way, as a fact of geology, was to them a gift of the land. What we might explain as necessity was for them another way of listening.

Perhaps there are clues in the other Early Bronze Age artifacts from the Cyclades. The bowls have small bases relative to the overhanging mass of their bodies. Their centre of gravity is high. They look unstable, but only if we think of them standing on a hard, flat surface. Imagine, instead, the bowl in the palm, or pressed down into sand on a beach. They nestle, like the figurines nestle.

If her arms were at her side, the hand could not encircle the waist.

The form invites holding.
The edges, tracing.

Every line could be situated with closed eyes.

The first roughing out required the eyes open.
The application of pigments required the eyes open.
And perhaps the incision of fingers and toes –

But the pure form, what the finger traces, what the eye traces –
This could have been made in darkness.

They used stone to make something visible.

      Cutting away –

      As each word said (– or not said)

   the first song was the sea

        obsidian came from an island called Melos
        struck – it gave blades

        the words they use in catalogues:
        prismatic, facet –

        and what's left after the striking:
        core –

        and the core taken then for other uses:
        burnish, grind –

        nothing wasted, ever–
        the sea journey remembered –

        the storms

Cycladic boats are believed to have had keels.[92]

M.W. Ovenden, writing in *The Philosophical Journal* in 1966, posited that the constellations were first named by sailors living on the Cycladic islands during the Early Bronze Age.[93]

In the same year, Michalis Bardanis, a teacher of mathematics living in the village of Apiranthos, on Naxos, published a study of Early Bronze Age marks on stones. He said they were symbols of constellations.[94]

Is there a figurine in the night sky?

        there is a cleft in the stone
        where life comes out

there is a cleft in the earth
where a body is given back

what runs from the body runs to the sea.

Episodes, discontinuous but linked and forward-moving – ?

Flowing around those episodes (as spirits around islands) –
voices, theories, fragments, facts – ?

Start with numbered episodes –
then gradually abandon the numbers – ?

(They are a sham, an illusion of structure and progress.)

I move from one side to the other, dodging my reflection in the glass.

And we will break with you.

> *Out of stone you came to us.*
> *Into stone you must return.*
>
> *But my children —*
> *my children's children!*
>
> *You will hear them running on the earth.*
> *You will hear them calling on the shore.*
> *You must not answer.*
> *Let them pass.*
> *(You must) let them pass.*

It would be hubris to think there was not a skein of stories behind the figurines, a mythology that ordered and consoled as thoroughly as any scripture.

> *We go with you*
> *always with you*

Is it a question of choice? Can we choose to dwell in the mythical?

To discuss meaning and function with archaeologists is to dwell in the realm of descriptive language. Books about the figurines describe them. Catalogues describe them. Read aloud, the descriptions have an incantatory power. *Incrustation, lyre-shaped, mottled, trapezoidal.* But their authority is illusory. The words add to the illusion that we know something more than we can see. They are a noise in the mind. Silencing the mind, abandoning the search for words and explanation, prepares us for another kind of knowing.

Frye again: *The most faithfully descriptive account of anything will always turn away from what it describes into its own self-contained grammatical fictions of subject and predicate and object.*[95]

After we have described the chemical composition of the pigment and the crystalline structure of the stone, we are no closer to penetrating the mystery of what the figurines meant to the people who made them, of how she helped them to live. Any other knowledge is lifeless.

Begin with an incantatory account of the launching of a ship – ?

(See Pound, *Canto 1*.)

Setting forth alone, a man with his mother's bones –

And a stirring lay upon the sea.

And the first song was the song of the sea.

I want this: that after a certain, ritualized period of time (three years? five? twenty?) the bones are moved – the grave is opened, and the bones are taken out and carried on board ship, wrapped in a skin; and with them the figurine that was buried with the body. And together they are taken to Keros, bones and figurine, and there the bones are taken into the cave and left, and outside the figurine is held up one last time to the sun and sky, and then is cast down hard upon the rocks. And the thread is broken to the dead. And the living go on, freed.

I want the pieces, not the whole. I want them left on Keros, not taken back to the islands they were borne away from in the night, at risk of shipwreck and drowning. The meaning is in the removal, and in the shattering, and in the abandonment, and in the place where this happened. Meaning is not a single note, but a song – from geologic upthrust to the first meeting of hand and stone, and then the bringing together of different stones in the hand, emery and marble, obsidian and marble, pumice and marble, each in its turn, and the form born again. And the form born again and again, over generations. And each figurine going to the grave with a human, and together removed, and together taken to Keros, and the bones left there, and the thread to the living broken, that the living may go on, free. And the figurine broken, symbolizing the breaking of the thread that once bound living and dead, mother and son, the necessity of letting go. The meaning is in the long song, culminating in the final disintegration of form, making room for new life and the rebirth of form.

We say they did not leave us writing, but they wrote meaning large, on the surface of their world. We say they had no written language but their loops and crosses, their cursive script, was their sea routes under sail and oar – from Melos bearing obsidian, from Thera bearing pumice, from Naxos bearing emery, and from all the isles, Siphnos and Kea, Syros and Amorgos, long reaches and tacks through straits with jagged shores – and this, in squall and current and storm.

Like landscape artists who walk great distances and leave barely a trace on the ground; like trappers running lines in a boreal winter; like the mandala of paths that monks walk on ridges dotted with cairns – there are other forms of writing on the world. We, with our books, are blind. The life cycle of the figurine, from geologic upthrust to female form, from life among the people to burial with the dead, from disinterment and journey to smashing and abandonment – there, perhaps, lies the great code of their meaning.

I am curled beneath a wild beast, a snake or a wild cat, scarcely breathing for fear it will strike. I am telling a story about how I will outwit the beast and survive. But I do not move. I can see the outline of its body and feel its weight pressing upon me. It is dark. I hear my mother coming down the hall and I call to her. My voice is tortured, my words ill-formed, an anguished cry of inarticulate need. I see her pass the open door, see that she has come from her bath and is wrapped in a white towel, her hair wet, her skin fresh and glowing. She is beautiful and young and radiant. But she is passing by – she does not hear me or see me. I cry louder, trying to will my thick tongue to form the word, like those with contorted faces who moan in the grip of a disease. She hears me! She turns back, and looks in, and sees me – and she comes to me. And the beast is no longer there pinning me, and she fills my view and she is beautiful. She raises her arm to me and the towel falls open, revealing her breast, the nipple young and full of promise. She covers herself again, and looks at me with tenderness and love, a benediction of love. But she does not take me in her arms, does not come that final step closer. And something turns in my understanding, though nothing is said, and I realize that she is saying goodbye to me, with all her love, she is going away from me, she is dying.

>I look again and again at the breaks
>what they reveal of the stone
>
>I look as we are drawn to look at what lies beneath the skin
>
>as, turning away from scenes of mutilation,
>we turn and look again
>
>We who never handle the bones of our dead

There is no continuity. We have no attachment.
There is boredom and there is greed.

We travel great distances quickly, unseeing, unfeeling, registering nothing.

plant the body

harvest the bones

Make the voyage to Keros the central section of the book – bookended, perhaps, by black pages?

Before – the struggle to break free of descriptive language.

After – light, illumination, a freer form ?

I am looking at things I cannot know.

There is this fear that saying anything will shatter what is essential.

the fire is cold
you must go now

birds must come back to us
fish must come back to us
spring must come back to us

you must go

> Voyage to Keros – a historical novel?
>
> The hope of the community is invested in the journey of a single man, returning his mother's bones to the underworld. This ritual is enacted annually for a woman who has died, by her first-born son, to ensure the continuity of the community.
>
> He makes the journey alone, by sea, by night, at the winter solstice, carrying her bones wrapped in her favorite skins. He must carry the bones into the cave on Keros, and say the words he has been taught to say, and leave them there, and then smash her figurine outside the cave. Then he must return alone by night, arriving at daybreak on his home island, bringing light and spring with him.

It hasn't rained in months. The earth is not so much earth as dust.

I know the proper word is *thirst*, but it feels like hunger.

We did not know then that things would not remain the same.

Frye: *A society, even one equipped with writing, cannot keep its central myths of concern constantly in mind unless they are continually being re-presented. The normal way of doing this is to associate them with ritual, setting apart regular intervals of sacred time when certain symbolic things are done....*[96]

      we expect her to speak
      we implore her –
      but why must she?

Frye also says that we shape our myths according to our human experience of birth and death – *because* we *begin and end, we insist that beginnings and endings must be much more deeply built into the reality of things than the universe around us suggests.*[97]

Letters home, to a woman I have loved – ?

(– and only later do I reveal that she's dead ?)

Or, each letter to a different woman – ?

Snake visits the graves
enters silently between the stones

curls among bones and limbs –
and then moves on.[98]

He makes notes, from books,[99] on classifications and divisions:

Archaeologists have divided the Early Bronze Age on the Cyclades into three periods, and further subdivided the periods into shorter phases. Distinctions are made on the basis of technological developments and changes in cemeteries and settlements.

The Early Cycladic I period began in 3200 BC and lasted 500 years. The period is divided into three phases, the Lakkoudes, the Pelos, and the Plastiras. These are the names of cemeteries on three different islands.

The Early Cycladic II period lasted about 400 years, from 2700 to 2300 BC. Settlements and cemeteries became larger, graves were used more than once. Two phases are distinguished: the Kampos phase, named after a site on Paros, and the Syros phase, named after the island itself. The Syros phase is the longest in Early Cycladic Culture. Towards the end of it, fortified settlements on high ground began to appear. Kastri was one.

The last period, Early Cycladic III, lasted two to three hundred years, ending around 2000 BC. There is only one phase, called Phylakopi I. By its end, Early Cycladic Culture had disappeared.

Archaeologists also classify the figurines into types, varieties, and sub-varieties. Different archaeologists have different systems. Tables have been drawn up linking the systems. Diagrams have been drawn showing changes in the figurines through time. Concordance tables align the catalogue and inventory numbers of museums and private collections.

I feel it sometimes in art museums, standing without moving before a single work – a Donatello, a Cézanne, a Giacometti – it could be anyone, anyone who has touched it, that instant of stillness, of revelation – revelation that Milosz says *will never advance beyond its beginning.*[100]

I should not ask for more.

> All the days of our lives, receding –
> stories, slipping back into the sea –

Who will remember us after the children have gone?

Pick up a stone.

> Do I need to better delineate genre boundaries – ?
>
> The protagonist speaks in poetry, in the present tense – ?
> (He is *in* the journey.)
>
> The narrator writes in prose, observing from a distance, or from above – ?

The archaeologists are trying to construct their own narrative – not who begat whom, but which culture begat the next. Seafarers swoop down out of the north, fortresses rise up in self-defence: a whole culture fighting for survival. And in the end, only the figurines survived. The rest, flesh of settlements, flesh of clans, knowledge of navigation and metallurgy and clay, all absorbed into the next phase, the next demarcation of time.

I was like an archaeologist, seeking evidence, accumulating facts, thinking: reason will triumph, description is enough.

But no: description is not enough.

Only myth will triumph, poetry.

and with the rock he slept
and into her let his manhood
go ...[101]

how to read the land

look for water, first –
then its course
downslope to the sea

the flatlands –
are they moist?
do they yield underfoot?
how thick the grasses?
how deep the loam?

study the sun –
its arc and sweep
what ground warmed?
what never touched?

climb the ridge –
turn your back to the wind
trace the lee slope to the shore
follow the drift of spume off the headland

light a smudge –
watch its drift
consider the odour of death
seeping from shallow graves

> Let the language oscillate, between poetic and descriptive – ?
>
> Until it becomes clear that the descriptive yields no insight, only peripheral knowledge –
>
> And so the poetic triumphs, and carries us forward – ?

time

ticking like a cellist's bow

Not all of the breaks were ritual or accidental.

Sometimes looters broke a large figurine, the easier to carry it.

In the Museum of Cycladic Art there is a large figurine that was cut by a saw, then broken in two.

A missing leg was found later in New York.

A conservator reassembled the body, reattached the leg.[102]

> He dies – ?
>
> The protagonist. He is meditating on death; it is all abstractions for him. We are expecting his mother to die. That's what he's afraid of.
>
> But instead it's he who dies.
>
> The narrator switches to the past tense – ?
>
> *If you look at his notebooks from the latter part of his journey....*

He is reading Willis and Tony Barnstone's critical introduction to the poems of Wang Wei:

"The transcendental sign that unifies nature for Wang Wei is distinguished from the Western sign in that in Buddhism the sign implies an absence, not a presence. Through the contemplation of the unity of all things, we may revert to that primordial absence...." [103]

There is something here, some clue – but what? Try it out –

There is both an absence, and a presence, in the figurines – an absence of individuality, a presence of – what?

The figurines imply a "primordial absence." They imply the presence of a unifying something (– a female spirit?) – but this presence is suggested, not stated. (Not *illustrated*, as Francis Bacon would say.[104])

Meaning is presented through absence. Meaning is *in* the absence.

The absence is a gift.

The absence of a written explanation is their gift to us.

– Or are these just words, pretty, interlocking words, signifying nothing?

> Try for another kind of voice, speaking directly of universals – ?
>
> Like *The Duino Elegies* ? Like Eliot's *Four Quartets* ?
> It feels too late now for anything else.
>
> And as Milosz wrote in his credo: it is time "to speak openly about all the things we do not understand."
>
> Czeslaw Milosz, "My Intention" (1969) in *Visions From San Francisco Bay,* trans. Richard Lourie (New York: Farrar, Straus and Giroux, 1975). Reprinted in Milosz, *To Begin Where I Am: Selected Essays,* ed. Bogdana Carpenter and Madeline G. Levine (New York: Farrar, Straus and Giroux, 2001), 2.

> The narrator's voice is the rational mind, the "vulgar" voice, the dead end of reason and science.
>
> The protagonist's voice emerges fitfully and slowly –
> we see glimpses of another way of looking –
> gradually it speaks more openly –
> culminates in a flowering of poetry and myth – ?
>
> An imagined Voyage to Keros then becomes a "narrative proposition" (Frye's term) in answer to questions which science and archaeology cannot answer.

They woke to the stench of decomposition.

They handled the bones of their parents.

Archaeology wants to remove mystery. It regards mystery as failure. But a sense of living within mystery is at the core of human religious experience.

Archaeology wants to know, but it won't allow knowledge to include awe. It won't allow knowledge to include not knowing. Certainty negates something essential.

The narrator registers events without interpreting them, removes his own self – ?

The protagonist changes from seeking explanation to acceptance of mystery – ?

Each episode includes an encounter with a woman – ?

Each woman is an aspect of First Woman – ?

After each episode, one more verse of the Voyage to Keros – ?

Each verse embodies the characteristics of the woman just encountered – ?

> Single-line poems – ?
>
> the purity of line equating with the line we trace with eye or finger –
>
> or
>
> Fragments of poems (like Sappho) – ?
>
> like shards, like pieces of broken figurines – ?

    I want to go silent
    read with my hands
    as lovers do.

    Song is born that way.

          I am belly
          I am cleft

He envisioned a regimen of disciplined craft, a clear line of work, the task set out in advance, his daily devotion to it leading steadily to completion and clarity. As simple as the story of a journey told from beginning to end. A daily work of craft that he could polish and refine until completed.

Instead, a chaos of indirection, unknowns, incompletions, unnameables.

He wanted a form as (apparently) simple as the form of the figurines. Left arm over right. Head tilted back. Feet pointed. Again and again.

Wanting to make something equal to her –

Distance myself – ?

"Observe, he is ..."

– and not just me, but all the men: Petros, the excavation workers, the Early Bronze Age man sailing to Keros.

Then, female voices – poetic, intuitive –

> voice of a figurine
> voice of the Early Bronze Age women, preparing the bones
> voice of the stone
> voice of the sea

The dead must move on.

Perhaps this is all we can say, the closest we can come to knowing:

Here they lived. Here are the beaches they pulled their boats up on. Here are the hills and mountains they walked on and hunted on, the slopes and lowlands where they planted seeds. This is what the world looked like.

But even this is speculation. Beaches migrate, cliffs collapse, rivers change course, springs stop flowing. What upthrusts, what collisions and breaks, have changed the islands over 4,000 years?

There's fear, too.
Fear of failure —
of being caught with nothing to say
or with saying something false.

Of not being equal to her.

A set of propositions, like Wittgenstein – ?

1.
1.1
1.11
1.12
1.13

1.2
1.21

This would evoke Wittgenstein's final proposition:
Whereof one cannot speak thereof one must be silent.

Ludwig Wittgenstein, *Tractatus Logico-Philosophicus*, trans. C. K. Owen (London: Kegan Paul, Trench, Trubner & Co., Ltd, 1922).

It's always there, gnawing at me, and the gnawing becomes more insistent and anxiety-inducing as time passes: Has my life been one long sham? If not *this* – this response to the thing held in my palm – then *what?*

A succession of journal entries – ?

The Broken Notebooks – ?

It's this looking for a form. If I had a form, then I could do it. Something I could fill, methodically, on a daily basis, my daily quota of work. That's all we ever want, isn't it? – a daily quota of work, something we can hold in our hands at the end of the day and say, look what I have made.

"In winter, bombs
came, making craters.
Nights –
we hid in the cemetery.

Graves lay open –
bones
were torn from the earth."

Letting go of form is a kind of dying, like letting go of the body – muscle and sinew fall away, the form falls apart.

> we have seen the pictures –
> the execution grounds
> the mass graves
>
> femur   rib   skull

>> *You must remember something!*
>> – No.
>> *Nothing at all?*

In asking for meaning, I know I'm asking the wrong question.

I look at the colour plate again, of the backlit figurine.
(I carry a photocopy with me still.)

I want to sink down against the marble skin – *pebbled* we call it, when it is human skin, taut with desire.

I want to lay against her. Her skin is an invitation to rest.

And inside her, mass, a reassurance that life will not end.

In Egyptian art, images of the pharaohs remained unchanged in formal structure for 3,000 years. The changes were in the depiction of individual features of the pharaohs. But the form, the precise and limited poses, remained unchanged.[105]

I have the facts, as many as I need. The rest I could get – but I don't want that. The facts are leading me away from something essential. The belief that facts will lead us to the other side, like stepping stones across ignorance – this belief dies hard. I cling to it still, to my notebooks, to the museum catalogues, to descriptions, as a survivor clings to flotsam. Words are like that, keeping us afloat.

> Monologues, dialogues – fleeting moments – ?

    prayers, if I had a god and knew his language

    songs, if I worked that way –

    songs from the chest, straining
    songs from the hands that carry stone

    songs stamped on the earth
    songs spinning on outstretched arms

    on keening

as Cecil Taylor danced around the piano –
a child's step dance, stooped
turning this way and that without preconceived form

He opens a book and looks at the pictures,[106] and after a while he records his thoughts:

They were capable of great plasticity, of sculpting beautiful limbs, of raising temporal flesh out of stone – the shift of a hip, the bend of a knee.

Look at Plate 155 – her long sensual legs, her hip slightly tilted, her buttocks firm, inviting caress. The author of the catalogue entry, Katie Dimakopoulou, says the carver "managed to surpass the usual rigidity and flat frontality of the Early Cycladic figurines." These are the words she employs:

> *slimness*
> *elegant*
> *graceful*
> *curvaceous*

She could have added *sensual, erotic*. They were capable, at least some of them were, and not just the unknown carver of the figurine in Plate 155. Look at the pregnant figurine in Plate 158. Look at Plate 162, the fragment of a seated male figurine. It's not that they couldn't do it, it's not that they didn't register the naked body as sensual. There was a conscious restraint. They chose to make, for a thousand years, an image of the body that transcends the short-lived beauty of youth.

Dimakopoulou wrote that the carver "managed to surpass the usual rigidity and flat frontality" but I see the inverse: the canonical figurines surpass the sensuality and temporality of the figurine in Plate 155 and the figurine in Plate 162 and the seated musicians and the other exceptions to the canon, exceptional as they are in their design and craftsmanship. The exceptions are descriptions, locked in time. The canonical figurines are the *poetic*, the mythic, transcending time. The exceptions are beautiful, remarkable, but they are secular images. The canonical figurines abstract the female body just enough to lift it beyond time, beyond the decay of flesh and the waning of desire, while still embodying something – what can we call it? – something essentially female?

I keep coming back to that something – what is it, that unnamable something I keep running up against? It's in my mind, not in the stone. It's in my need to name, to articulate, to fix in words, when everything about her says, let go – stop clinging – there are no words that will ever suffice – this is beyond flesh now, beyond the span of one person's life, beyond the lust that draws us together for a fleeting instant, this is beyond flesh, beyond dying, beyond the grave, beyond memory, beyond the memory of one lifetime, or the lifetimes of those we remember – this is beyond the one and the many –

lie still
lie still

What they made was equal to the world.[107]

Once there were hearth fires and a ribbon of smoke carried the scent of cooking to the graves on the hill.

Now, the hills are burning, the air is acrid. The taste of death is in our throats.

Tourists wander through galleries, holding smart phones, taking pictures.

– *Do you know nothing?* [108]

but if we sit with them –

still, and still moving[109]

a perception that cannot be articulated
an ear that, having heard, cannot replicate the sound

a bowl
a shoreline

a 12-bar blues

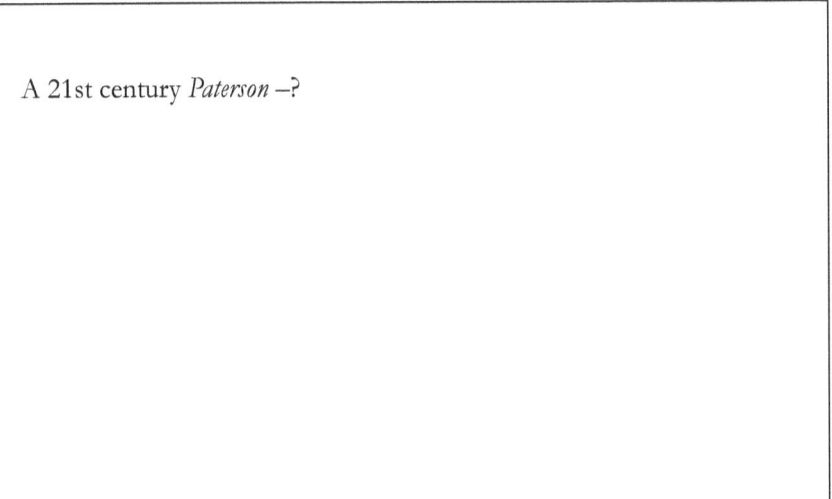

A 21st century *Paterson* –?

I cannot see her. Our bodies are diffuse. She collapses on the bed beside me – vaguely she is in my arms – vaguely she is surrendering.

And then she is gone.

        4.1
        4.11
        4.111
        4.112
        4.1121

Who are you?
What do you look like?

I am a man.
I want to see.

what do I do with these impulses, these yearnings
these very words, slipping through –

        a woman, putting on make-up before a mirror
        her hair wet and heavy from the bath
        pulls a white robe closed across her breast

I feel more acutely than ever the agony of having nothing to hold.

I imagine structures, but feel no urgency to fill them.

I imagine a long, formless poem, segueing organically from key to key, voice to voice, inner to outer – an open-ended, endlessly metamorphosing poem –

        as conversation unfolds

        as *riverrun*[110] –

But nothing holds.

She wasn't made for words.

        We will be here.
        We will always be here.

Gratitude to the worm.

Gratitude to the microbe and the rain.

> As Mingus performed – ?
>
> Stay where you are until you're ready to move on –

The graves came closer to the surface as the topsoil washed away.

Bones still turn up on battlefields.

We will be here.
We will always be here.

We will go with you.
Do not be afraid.

    as speech is formless
    as history is formless
    until marks are made on a page

    left arm over right
    head tilted back

    she dipped a finger and pulled out blue

Transcript: Olga Philaniotou, archaeologist.[111]

When I look at the broken pieces of figurines that were found on Keros, I find them moving, in a strange way – because of the possibility that they were deliberately broken, as part of a ritual. Why do you put the figurines back together again?

Why not put them back together again?

Perhaps some of the meaning, or message, of the fragments is lost when you reassemble them.

Archaeology tries to reconstruct the period – so you try to reconstruct objects. Look at the Parthenon: should we have left it lying on the ground in pieces? The prevailing idea is to repair it, to bring back some of the original glory of it. Some archaeologists do believe that what we see today has been created by history, and so we should leave it as it is. But I don't. Anyway, the Keros fragments will never be fully reconstructed. Only a few matching pieces have been found.

4,000 years of remembering in these hands

the fish I killed with a blow to the head
the body roasted on the fire

        Moon of the Heavy Net
        Moon of the Full Basket

                                      wind
                                    carry our song

what the ancient Egyptians carved:
    sandstone
    black granite
    quartzite
    alabaster

    here –

        marble

        bones of the land

and the dead themselves are getting up and coming to the living.[112]

        history conceals from us
        what has always been there

        and what will be there still
        after we are gone

She never sleeps in a man's arms.

It is she that leaves the bed
she that comes back in the morning

(or not at all).

        death releases us from the claims of the living

        death cleanses us

        death frees us from our demons and our needs

> Employ irony?
>
> The narrator mocks the protagonist's earnestness,
> doesn't take seriously his stutters of poetry and confession –
>
> Eventually, the protagonist rebels, fires the narrator –
>
> And then – ?

The folded arms offer nothing –

> The narrator might say: "We cannot be privy to his thoughts or feelings, but we are allowed to imagine, so I will."

> The narrator could say at the outset:
>
> "I can't promise that reading this book will lead you to any satisfactory end."

Story is ending before our eyes –

>> we need answers, however small
>> we need gods we can hold on to

elements which appear alien come together: soon a strange form moves in circles...[113]

> Not pure *automatisme*, but *automatiste* techniques to raise the mythic – ?

He thinks again of absence –

The forests that once covered the islands: oak, he wants them to be, so he can think of acorns and say the word *mast*, the fallen fruit.

He thinks of deer, wild boar, the plump game birds (gone).

Whole species (gone).

He thinks of topsoil, washed to the sea.

Land formations, estuaries, cliff faces.

Songs and dances, each with a name.

He thinks of the old Jewish cemetery in the Grosse Hamburger Strasse.

He thinks of a room, open to the sky.[114]

collective ancestry, not just individual ancestors –

(as Abdullah Ibrahim reminds us)

        we assemble words
        we assemble lives

        we put on words –

        clay on an armature

We see her blank face as form, perhaps as symbol. They may have seen it as prepared surface, ready to take paint.

The blank surface confounds us; it confronts us. It points to a place before the book, before, even, the symbol or phoneme chiseled in stone.

We are on a vast plateau, sloping to the sea.

> More and more it must become an imaginary place.

    and there was fire, tended and artfully guarded
    and at night, a circle
    and voices, raw with winter cold

    and there was flute and drum and clapping
    children's hands enclosed within their mothers' –

        wide-eyed, mesmerized

        fish dancing before their eyes

I cannot sleep. I cannot leave you. Can someone help me? I'm so tired.[115]

Begin with nothing, only white expanse – ?

But without words, how will anyone hear him – ?

Totally deconstruct – ?

Narrator: "This is what we are given: 4 field notebooks, 5 private journals, 8 monographs, a museum booklet, a few photocopied articles and pages from other books, a few colour photocopies of plates from books, 2 marble samples, his memory."

Allow the narrator only a descriptive voice – ?

> *This is taking place ...*
>
> *This is being said ...*
>
> *He is doing this ...*

Just lists and propositions – ?

A book of propositions – ?

(But this is hopelessly pedantic.)

> Bone is structure to the body.
> So make the human skeleton structure to the story – ?
>
> (What story – ?)
>
> Limit my numbered propositions to the exact number of bones in the human skeleton – ?

> Insert more structure cards – ?
>
> A flurry of them, a desperate grasping after form – ?

Blood, flowing like water.[116]

He copied the words into his notebook, thinking there must be a way to continue this – and then white was all he remembered, hurting his eyes.

We are on board the *Romilda*. It's getting dark. The sea is choppy, with whitecaps and spume.

I'm travelling with Olga Philaniotou, the government archaeologist responsible for the Cycladic islands, including Keros. She travels continually between Athens and the islands, sleeping in rented rooms, getting up before dawn to keep up with paper work. She often works seven days a week. She is 61.

Three years ago, Olga had thirteen people working for her on Naxos alone. They were involved in excavations, conservation, photography, documentation, and running the archaeological museum. Now she has only one full-time employee, Daphne Lalayannis, the museum's conservator.

One of Olga's responsibilities is approving building permits on the Cycladic islands, which means she must inspect every site to see if it has archaeological significance. If she thinks it may, she organizes the digging of a trial trench or pit. If that indicates value, she undertakes a "rescue excavation." State funding for archaeology has been so drastically cut that she can't hire enough people to do the excavations efficiently. She is currently supervising three rescue excavations on three different islands. A rescue excavation can take up to five years. We are on our way to see one, on Pano Kouphonisi.

The best way to do archaeology, she says, *is to excavate a little, study what you find, publish the results, then go back and excavate some more. But rescue excavations don't have the luxury of time. Landowners are impatient. You have to learn what you can quickly, save what you can, then get out and allow building to go ahead. An excavation is like a book you can read only once – then it's burned. There's no going back for another look.*[117]

The ship stops at another island en route. The pier is at the end of a narrow inlet between steep rocky shores. There are no lights, no buoys, no room for error. The captain executes a 180-degree turn in the passage and backs to the pier. In five minutes the ferry has unloaded and loaded and cast off ropes. As we pull away, men with fishing rods reclaim their positions on the pier. Then we are back out to sea and darkness enfolds us.

The next day: The peninsula slopes down gently on one side, to a sheltered cove. The opposite, uphill side ends in a sheer, 30-metre drop to a pebble beach. Olga shows me the trial pits they dug a few years ago at the top of the slope. One pit ends in thin air. The cliff face is unstable and still being eroded by the sea. Olga believes that during the Early Bronze Age the land extended much further and there was a settlement here. She points out blackened earth and stone in one pit. She says this may be either organic matter, or residue from a fire; they don't know yet. She says there's no way to know how far the settlement extended. About a kilometre away, on a hillside, is an Early Bronze Age cemetery.

The new dig is halfway down the slope towards the cove, in the middle of a field. There are five fields on the slope, separated by low stone walls. There's a chicken coop in the top field, near the old test pits. The lower fields show signs of ploughing, but there are no crops. The earth is strewn with sherds of clay pottery. Olga says this is one indication that the site is worth exploring.

The new pit is about three metres square. It's only a few centimetres deep so far. It's marked out by yellow cord stretched between steel rods driven into the ground at the corners. Yellow tags flutter from the rods. Nearby are six shallow trenches, each about three metres long, intersecting one another at various angles. Two of the trenches are new. Olga says they are digging here to see how far down the slope the settlement extended. The field below us has more steel rods driven into it, for more trenches.

He raises the pick to the height of his boot top, then lets it drop of its own weight. He pulls a clump of earth away. He turns the pick on its side and taps the clump lightly, breaking it open. He sees something. He works his fingers through the earth, pulls out a sherd, and tosses it into a plastic basin on the ground. He works alone, bent double, moving forward incrementally. Then he steps out and Shovel steps in.

Shovel doesn't open new ground. He scoops up the earth that Pick left behind, leaving the patch of ground clean and level and smooth. He tips the earth from his shovel into a wheelbarrow, watching it fall. When he's finished, he steps out, and Pick steps back in.

Barrow watches intently. His job is to wheel the earth to the edge of the field, dump it in a prearranged location, and return quickly. He watches every scoop of earth going into his barrow. When Pick overlooks a sherd, and Shovel misses it, too, Barrow pulls it out and shows it to the others. If they nod, he leans forward and places it in the basin.

Pick is top dog, the most experienced worker on the site. He handles his tools, a large pick and a smaller, short-handled one, with precision and delicacy. He spits on his palms to keep a sure grip on the handle. He spots sherds the size of pebbles. He doesn't talk much while he's in the pit. He doesn't smoke. He wears an insulated nylon jacket over an olive-green army sweater, clean jeans, work boots, and a blue toque. His moustache is trimmed. He's in his 50s.

Shovel is close in age to Pick. He's more playful and gregarious, but he knows his place. When there's room, he sometimes steps into the pit and starts his clean-up while Pick is still working. But he always stands behind Pick. He never touches earth that Pick hasn't stepped over. Shovel wears clean jeans, too, and an insulated jacket, but no hat. He smokes while he works.

Barrow is the youngest. Shovel tells him where to place his wheelbarrow and when to empty it. Barrow is deferential. His boots are worn. His thick olive green cargo pants are faded. He wears two sweaters, no hat. He smokes the least and talks hardly at all.

Supervising them is an archaeologist in his thirties. He doesn't touch the pick, shovel, or barrow. He has his own small trowel and brush. His other tools are to one side: surveying equipment, tape measures, a chalkboard, a digital camera, notebooks and pens, tags and cords and clear thick plastic bags. Archaeologist stands at the edge of the pit. He gives directions when necessary, and occasionally puts one foot in and scrapes at the earth. But he knows his place, too, knows the men don't need to be told how to do their jobs. Archaeologist is dressed in city clothes: his cargo pants are lightweight and clean, his shirt tails hang out below a black corduroy jacket. He wears a fanny pack, pouch to the front, with his cell phone inside. He has a leather shoulder bag, too, set down nearby.[118]

Olga is the lead archaeologist, but she can't always be on site. She decides the future of the excavation, its duration, its financing, its pace. She decides where to dig and how deep to go. She comes and goes all day between meetings with the landowner and the municipal authorities. When she's at the site she observes, asks questions, decides, directs. She shares cigarettes and good-humoured banter with the crew. She doesn't touch a tool.

They have finished the first layer. They stretch a red cord across the pit, from top to bottom, dividing it in half. They resume digging on the left side of the cord. When they have gone down a few more centimetres and the demarcation is clearly visible in the earth, they remove the cord and carry on.

They're down 25 centimetres now on the uphill side of the pit, and finding lots of sherds. When the basin is full, they empty it into a clear plastic bag. Archaeologist writes something on a yellow tag and places it inside the bag, facing out. He shows me some of the sherds.
– How do you know it's Early Bronze Age?
He shows me a pottery lip.
– The material tells us.

I tell Olga I'm amazed that these sherds were lying less than 30 centimetres underground for 4,000 years, and were never disturbed. She says farming practices have changed little on these small islands and many farmers still use "primitive" ploughs that only dig down a few centimetres into the earth.

Across the road from the excavation site there are two new buildings. They look like small apartment complexes. Each building has three or four units. At peak season they will bring the owner a handsome income. They are built on a slope of land, with a view of the cove and the sea and neighbouring islands. Keros is visible, and the rugged south coast of Naxos. There are air conditioners on the outside walls of the buildings and TV antennas on the roofs. A new stone wall surrounds the property, topped with concrete. Inside, the land is terraced and planted with cacti, palms, and shrubs.

Just down the road from the buildings, where the land levels out to the cove, unwanted things have been dumped over an old wall. There's a moped, lying on its side, and an old boat engine. There's a mattress, a smashed wooden row boat, and an entire fishing boat, it's steel propeller and tiller hanging in the air, the wood hull rotting. Across the road, at the shore of the cove, is a small stone house with a flat roof. Outside, an old man and woman are sitting, their faces to the sun.

Pick is bent double. He has a short-handled pick in one hand and a brush in the other. He's cleaning the soil from a row of rocks that he has uncovered. Archaeologist is writing notes. Pick steps out, lets Shovel clean up. Pick contributes a little banter while waiting, then steps back in and resumes work. He uses his brush to nudge open a clump of earth he has loosened. Archaeologist steps in, Pick steps aside. Archaeologist prods and brushes for a moment, then steps out again.
– What is it?
– Just rock.
Archaeologist takes me to one of the nearby trenches and shows me five stones bunched tightly together, about 15 centimetres below ground, running uphill towards the pit.
– A wall?
– We don't know yet. We must dig.

The crew have finished another layer. The music of pan pipes fills the air and Archaeologist pulls out his cell phone. When he's finished the call, he tells the crew to move their tools away from the pit. They clean up the site, brushing pebbles off the surrounding ground. Archaeologist writes something on the chalkboard and lays it in the pit. Beside it he places a white arrow with a red point on it, to indicate north. He props up the chalkboard with a stone, so the text is more visible. He orders Barrow to bring the wheelbarrow to the edge of the pit and hold it steady, then climbs in to take a picture. His body casts a shadow over the pit, evoking laughter and teasing from Pick and Shovel. Archaeologist gets out, turns the chalkboard around, and moves with Barrow to the other side of the pit. He takes several photos. He gets out, the barrow is moved aside, and Shovel steps into the pit with a surveyor's pole. Archaeologist moves to a tripod set up nearby and takes a sighting with a precision instrument. He makes more notes. Without waiting to be told, the crew resumes digging.

Archaeologist chides Pick to go slower. He gets into the pit and uses his trowel to scrape at something. Pick disputes there's anything there. He's right. Archaeologist steps aside. Pick resumes. Archaeologist stays in the pit, brushing a rock at the edge. Barrow stoops and picks up a sherd that has fallen on the ground, examines it, and puts it in the basin. Pick and Shovel are bantering. The pace is picking up. Everyone seems more focussed, as if they are expecting something. Archaeologist uses his trowel and brush to clean around a stone. The others work around him. They've been excavating for three hours now, without a break. They are running on early morning coffee and a steady ingestion of nicotine.

Another 30 minutes, another layer. They stop, attach tape measures to the rods at the top and bottom corners on the left side of the pit. They draw out the tapes to meet at the midpoint on the opposite side. Archaeologist takes a reading and makes more notes.

– What is it?

He shows me two obsidian blades, each about four centimetres long.

– From Melos?

– Yes.

– What do you write on the label?

– Exact – where we find them – the depth.

– Is it good?

– We find a lot.

He points to the pit, indicating he must get back. The crew are working quickly.

Pick and Shovel are both in the pit. Shovel is behind Pick. Suddenly, Shovel emits a loud cry: *ooooahhhh!* He picks up something from the loose earth that Pick has stepped over. Archaeologist rushes over and asks to see it. Shovel taps the object several times in the palm of his hand, trying to dislodge the dirt. Then he hands it over. Archaeologist examines it and lays it on the ground outside the pit, beside the place where it was found. They bring out the tape measures. Archaeologist makes notes. Shovel picks up the object again – it's a sea shell – and pretends to talk into it like a cell phone. Archaeologist chides him with a smile, then goes to the tripod and takes a sighting. Quickly they go back to digging, Pick first, but using the small trowel now.

    – What did you find?
    – From the sea. Early Bronze Age. We must wash it.
    – A tool?
    – No. I think for eat.
    – Old?
    – Yes!
    – How do you know?
    – Like stone.

With broken English and gestures, he communicates that minerals in the soil have turned the shell to a stone-like hardness, like petrified wood.

Barrow is observing intently, crouched at the edge of the pit. Archaeologist looks into the wheelbarrow, runs his fingers through the dirt, and pulls out five sherds. He taps Barrow on the shoulder, passes the sherds to him, and indicates the basin.

Olga and I are walking behind the others, to a taverna. It's time for a midday meal. I ask her about the workers. Pick and Shovel have been with her for 20 years. You start as a barrow-man, she says, and learn by watching. Barrow is not allowed to touch any tools. It's too dangerous, for the excavation and the artifacts. When Olga thinks he's ready, he'll be allowed to try the shovel. You may spend years on the shovel before graduating to the pick. Handling the pick is "the height of achievement." Shovel came to her as a young man. His father worked for her, too. Pick and Shovel have enormous knowledge, she says. "They know things the young archaeologist doesn't know yet."

Olga and Archaeologist are sitting on the ground, their feet in the pit, watching intently. The others are digging. Olga and Shovel keep up a steady banter. I approach, crouch down, ask Olga how deep they will go.
– Until they reach virgin soil.
– What's that?
– Where there are no antiquities, no human presence.
– How far down is that?
– They don't know until they get there. It could be 50 centimetres – or 50 metres.

Two men approach across the field. There's a buzz of conversation and significant glances. Olga stands up and talks to the newcomers for a few minutes, then they leave. More significant glances. I wonder whether it's the landowner, anxious to know if they're finding anything, and how much longer he'll have to wait for his building permit. Olga says it's the son of the landowner and his friend. She offered to hire them, but they weren't interested. She says she can't find two workers on the island who are willing to work for her.

A few minutes later, a young teenage boy arrives in sweat pants and a hoodie. He knows the crew; his grandfather owns the taverna. The crew tease him. He goes to the barrow, pulls something out of the dirt, and shows it to Archaeologist. Archaeologist crumbles it; it's just dirt. The boy digs in again and this time pulls out a real sherd that the others have missed. He hands it to Archaeologist. Archaeologist tosses it into the basin. The boy sits down with his feet inside the pit, just like Olga. Archaeologist shoos him out. The boy leans on Pick, who's standing at ease while Shovel works. Everyone is smiling, they enjoy his presence. He asks questions, shows interest in their work. Throughout it all, the excavation never stops. Barrow crouches at the edge of the pit, watching the earth intently. They're thigh-deep into the hillside now.

In the absence of anything else – facts.

When he feels like something is slipping away – facts.

If nothing else – an accumulation of facts.

The human body contains more than 200 bones.[119]

Bones are a composite: 70 per cent mineral, 30 per cent organic. The mineral content, a form of calcium phosphate, gives bone its rigidity. The organic content, mainly a protein called collagen, allows bones to flex, giving them resilience and strength. The organic content breaks down after death, which is why the bones of the dead become brittle.

Bone appears to be lifeless; in fact, it is living tissue. Bone is permeated by nerves and blood vessels. Bone is continually being formed and broken down. Bone can repair itself.

There are differences between the bones of men and women. The pelvis is the most reliable clue. The narrow pelvis of the male is suited for locomotion. The broad pelvis of the female enables child-bearing. Generally, the bones of the male are bigger and thicker.

Bones attached to one another make a skeleton. The skeleton provides structure for the body.

After death, the body decomposes. Bones and teeth are the last to go. While the bones themselves may endure thousands of years, the tissues that held them together decompose. Look at an old skeleton uncovered in a grave: the form of the body is visible, but the bones are no longer attached to one another and, if disturbed, the form falls apart.

Our lives have form. Our stories support our identity. Like bones, the stories that make up our lives are living things: they grow and break and rebuild themselves. But as we grow old, the structure breaks down, our memories break down, until we are left with only pieces. Order falls apart – what happened first, what happened next, what she said that cut so deep.

How to excavate a skeleton:

Keep it intact.
Remove soil carefully with a paint brush and dental tools.
Do not disturb the position of the bones.
Photograph the exposed skeleton.
Make notes.
Then, lift the bones out gently.
Keep them together, separate from the bones of adjacent skeletons.
Sieve the remaining soil in the grave, especially from the areas around the hands and feet, to recover small bones, bone fragments, and loose teeth that may have been overlooked.[120]

Every corpse must be disposed of.

Some ways this has been done:

>   slipped into rivers
>   exposed to the sky, in trees or on platforms
>   abandoned, to be eaten by wild animals
>   buried
>   burned[121]

Listen for the wingbeat of a passing bird.

Listen for a howl at dusk –

Two distinct processes are involved in the decomposition of the human body.

First, when the body dies, enzymes inside the cells begin breaking down the same tissue that they previously helped build and maintain. The process is called *autolysis*, meaning self-digestion.

Second, bacteria inside the stomach and intestines that once helped digest food change from having a symbiotic relationship with the body to becoming parasitic: they begin eating the body itself. This is called *putrefaction* and this is what causes the odour of death. The belly swells and bursts from the gases produced by the work of the bacteria. Eventually, bacteria from the surrounding soil and air also feast on the corpse, and fungi, insects, and larvae move in for their share.

Eventually, the flesh of the body is completely converted into soil and air.

In temperate climates, it takes about ten years for an adult body to be reduced to a bare skeleton in a grave. But the time needed varies, depending on:
1. the climate;
2. the length of time between death and burial;
3. the depth of burial;
4. the composition of the soil –
the more acidic the soil, the faster the decomposition;
5. the availability of water and oxygen;
6. the clothing and coffin materials;
7. how much fat there is on the body;
8. whether the body is that of an adult or a child –
children decompose twice as fast.

Some parts of the body decompose faster than others. Hair is highly resistant to decomposition, because of the keratin in it. Ligaments and tendons are slow to decay because they contain collagen. Bones may last thousands of years. The enamel on teeth is the most resistant of all: teeth may be found even when all the bones are gone.

The decomposition of the bones is a complex process. Micro-organisms from the soil (fungi, bacteria, algae) break down the organic matter in the bones. This creates acidic byproducts which in turn dissolve the minerals in the bones.[122]

Some aboriginal societies regard all archaeological research as racist, and all prehistoric sites as sacred.

Some archaeologists have agreed to rebury bones, and even photographs of the bones.

Other archaeologists argue that preservation of skeletons is a professional duty, and that destruction or reburial is equivalent to the destruction of a single-copy manuscript.[123]

> *We know them when they come.*
> *We warm them by the fire.*
>
> *We take them under our skins when we sleep.*
> *We listen to their song in the night.*

She leads him to a room below ground, a place of long aisles with white fluorescent tubes overhead. She gestures down a row of metal shelves on which are stacked identical, grey cardboard boxes, their ends numbered by hand in black ink.

"May I look?" he says, pointing from his eye to a box. He gestures open.

She walks slowly down the aisle, considering something, then stops and reaches above her head and pulls out a box. She carries it on her forearms to a bare table in the centre of the room. She slides the box off her arms and positions it at the centre of the table, then lifts off the cover and steps aside.

He is gripped by something we cannot know. He is silent. The attendant is silent. (Darkness is falling outside.) He steps forward and looks down into the box. We hear him exhale. The attendant watches him. Slowly he reaches into the box and lifts out a femur. He holds it in front of him in his open palms. It is cool and light (this much we are allowed to know). He remains motionless for several minutes. We hear him murmur something, under his breath.

"Sorry?" she asks, leaning forward. He does not answer or look at her. He continues looking at the bone. She watches him, her mouth twisting slowly at the corner. She waits a moment longer, then steps forward with the lid, looks at him, and inclines her head toward the open box.

What songs did they sing?

        Song of the chipping stone.
        Song of the cutting stone.
        Song of the thirsty stone.

How many times did they repeat the song?

        Till the form came free.

Where are the bones while they sing?

        On the hill.

Are they waiting?

        Yes.

Are they singing, too?

        [silence]

        [wind]

I went to her alone

I sat with her alone
waiting for her to speak

I traced (with my eye) the outline of her –

　　　　　as a palm traces an absent hip
　　　　　as Gary Snyder sang a distant ridge
　　　　　as Cézanne studied Mont Sainte-Victoire

　　　　　moving his easel from field to field
　　　　　through long years of attending

In order to render visible the quintessence of things, the external form of the motif is simplified.[124]

No voice, never a voice, never a story
only borrowed words, borrowed stories –

Something cracks when I reach for it.

What hope is there in this?

　　　　　　　　　　I have a sense of disappearing, dissolving
　　　　　　　　　　into silence and white –
　　　　　　　　　　just a Bach chorale prelude
　　　　　　　　　　BWV 639, transcription by Kempff –

　　　　　　　　　　and the long line of the sea, unmoved

It should be all right to say I don't know, I don't quite know, I can't quite put a word to it. I remind myself of that. But it feels like failure.

And given this now, the endless arc of the sea, where do I fix my words?

Here, on this line, in the order stipulated by the inherited grammar of my language?

Outside, there, where the sea turns between continents – with what words, in what language do I speak?

Hold fast in the face of this blankness.[125]

>
> as seasons repeat
> as generations repeat

Hold fast.

Senior monks in a Buddhist monastery read the depth of a junior monk's practice by the clatter he makes in the kitchen – the rattled dishes, the efficiency of his work, the wastage. Perhaps breakage of a figurine during the making was a similar measure: a moment's distraction, too much haste or force, and one had to start again.

The figurines that we see in museums represent the culmination of years of practice. The total number of figurines in the world are only a portion of the figurines that were started. Therein, perhaps, lies their power. They are distillation.

>
> each attempt at the form was reaching for an absolute
> each variation, a rebirth
>
> the stillness in the form
> was stillness earned
>
> grain by grain

May I touch?

I am a man.

I need to touch.

He has a theory. Let us allow him this. (And why not? There is so much that will never be known.) He believes the figurines were carved by blind men, perhaps men who had been ritually blinded and thereby accorded special status. It stands to reason, he thinks: the form is so simple, pared to an essential outline; there are almost no details, none that require sight to situate. The master carvers, he theorizes, began as sighted apprentices, young men chosen by the community on the basis of some predilection or inner light. Or, perhaps apprenticeship was a rite of passage for all young men. These apprentices roughed out the form, in pieces of raw marble brought to the master's workshop by the old women of the island: this was the old women's role in the community, to visit the veins of raw marble and select the stones. In this way, he theorizes, those who had once brought life into their midst now brought an embodiment of death, raw white stone that was the bones of the land and the bones of their ancestors, one and the same. They handed the stone to the boys who were becoming men, to give it new life. The apprentices learned by trial and error, and from the example of the older apprentices: words were used sparingly. In this way the young men learned perseverance, patience, attention, care – attributes that would serve them well in hunting, tilling, boat-building, navigation. The young men learned to see and to observe shape, form, flaw. They learned to smell impurities in the stone, listen for forewarnings of breakage. Inattention, clumsiness, too much force, and the stone broke and had to be discarded, with the knowledge that the work of an old woman, who had carried the stone to them from the hills or the beach, had been wasted by their inattention and haste.

Many stones broke, many others were rejected by the blind master at any stage in the chipping and grinding of the apprentices. The form not right, the balance off; the quality in the stone that had drawn the old woman's eye, defiled – the master felt the failure in his hand and silently rejected it. That was the practice and the way. The spirit link to the body of the land must not be broken. In this way, through repetition, observation, and rejection, laborious slow service to the blind master taught all young men of the community reverence for their land, their women, their dead, their story. It taught them stillness and attention. It taught them to listen. From the master they also learned the songs and stories of their place, and learned how to address the stone. Over time (he has no theories about how long; their time was not our time, he thought, inconceivable to us) – over time, some young men demonstrated a gift or a calling and were allowed to continue. The others returned to the everyday work of the community, humbled, trained in the ways of the spirit, knowing the songs and stories of their world.

The older apprentices took the emerging form from the younger apprentices and further refined it, submitting it again and again to the blind carver for the judgment of his hands. At any stage a figurine could be rejected – at any time, through loss of attention, the link to the hands of the old woman who chose the stone, and through her to the land and the dead who lay buried in it – at any time, this link might be broken and the carving become lifeless, a sacrilege. The blind master felt it. He sat in judgment, not with his eyes but with his hands and his spirit and his song. He sang the song to each form handed to him. When a form pleased the song, the song continued to its end; more often, it stopped, and he handed the stone back. When the song continued to its end, the master then held the stone a long time in silence, listening. The apprentices listened with him. When he was sure the form was ready, he nodded toward the apprentice who had given it to him it, stood up, and carried the stone to his private room. There, with tools no one else was allowed to touch, he gave the figurine its final texture and life.

His theory extends itself into a story he would like to recite, but can only imagine. – The blind master finishes the figurines by touch alone, remembering through his hands the dead body of his mother, that he carried to the grave, remembering the dry bones of his mother that he lifted out years later in preparation for the journey. For the blind master is the one who made the journey to Keros, taking the bones of his mother to the island of the dead. He is the one who unwrapped the bones and lay them in the cave among the other bones. He is the one who set her free, raising the figurine that had lain with her in the grave high above his head and letting it fall on the rocks outside the cave. The memory of that is in his hands. He remained on Keros alone, sleeping at the mouth of the cave, listening, fasting, until the first birds came back and the sun came back and his song was born. And then he slaughtered the goat he had brought with him, that had nourished him with milk during his vigil, and he roasted her body over fire and ate her. His strength renewed, he sailed home, bringing with him the sun and the birds and the fish that swam under his boat. And he brought with him his song, the words that had been given to him, that renewed and extended the song of his people, the song without end.

It is his last spring of sightedness, his last journey by sea. It is the last time he will be guided by the stars, the last time the sun will dance on the water for him, and the white throat of the birds flash for him. When he returns to his island there is rejoicing, and the sun and the birds and the fish are brought ashore with him. The days lengthen, and grow warmer. He speaks to no one about what he has seen. One night he submits to the glowing poker, and the sun embraces him one last time; he cries aloud in pain, and crosses over to the land of darkness.

> *the sea's breathing was calm*
> *the sea was resting*
>
> *his cry woke up the night*
>
> *it woke up the moon*
> *it frightened the stars*

He is ministered to carefully, attentively, his every need anticipated and met – the choicest meats, milk from a breast, the first serving of grain. When he is strong again, and his wounds have healed, he goes to the fire where the others have gathered, and he sings the long line of their song, from its distant beginning, the line that comes down to them from their ancestors. And when he reaches the end, he adds the words that were given to him on Keros, and the words reassure them that they are not forgotten. And they are released from death again, and sing his praises, and dance for him all night at the fire.

When he wakes he is taken to where the apprentices wait, where he himself once waited.

Henceforth, his life was devoted to the figurines and the story. He alone sang the whole story. He alone was allowed to sing the story to the figurine, giving it to her to hold. He was living proof of her power to bring stillness, for it was only by stillness that a figurine could be finished without breaking its connection to the ancestors and the land. In this way, the figurine became an embodiment of the mystery. When it was finished, it was given to the community. There was some process for deciding who would be entrusted with its care, or who needed most to hold it; (he has no theory about that).

The figurine was adorned, painted with hair and eyes and mouth, allowing it to move easily among them. In this way, the bones of the ancestors and the bones of the land took human form again, and lived among them again for a while, before returning to the earth in the grave.

This he knows to be true, though he cannot say how he knows.

As a young boy I sat with my playmates around an old wooden cartwheel half-buried in a field near my home. We knew – we did not speculate – we knew that a magic story book was buried under the hub of the wheel. We didn't know what the stories were about, no one did, but we knew there was a book of them, buried under the wheel. We never, in my memory, tried to dig it up. It was only sand, it would have been an afternoon's adventure to uncover the wheel and drag it aside. We never did. We came to that place often, and sat around the wheel, resting from our play, and we talked about the book. No one had seen it, no one knew how it had gotten there, but no one questioned its existence. The wheel and the book were part of the cosmology of our world.

No one knows where the gods begin – on what night, around what fire. But surely they are spoken into life.[126] A child makes something sacred to his world, without knowing the origin. So Keros became sacred to the Early Bronze Age inhabitants of the Cyclades, and no one will ever know why. There are no letters incised in stone to tell us, there are only the routes of the sailors who journeyed to Keros, routes like an invisible mandala upon the sea. The message left to us is in the waves and the stars, and in the shattered figurines they left behind on the island. Joining the pieces is brushing away footprints.

> give me the bones of my mother
> let me wash the bones of my mother
> let me carry them in my arms
>
> let me navigate storms with them
> let me navigate death
> let me arrive, at dawn
>
> let me do that much for her

Yourgos slows at the crest so I can admire the view. Despotiko is spectacular in the bright sunshine, across a narrow strait. There are a handful of white buildings close to the shore – a chapel and some farm buildings – but Yourgos says no one lives there anymore. A few farmers go across to tend fields and graze sheep and goats. The coastal strip is flat, but beyond that the island crinkles into ridges and rocky peaks. The highest is less than 200 metres, but the rise is so abrupt it gives the impression of greater height.

We drop down to the shore and stop at a wharf. Two boats are tied up. A woman is descaling a catch of small fish, scraping them with a kitchen knife and rinsing them in the sea. Yourgos talks to her, then heads off towards a taverna. I start to follow, but he tells me to wait. He returns in a few minutes with a young man who leads the way to a fibreglass boat with an outboard motor.

By now I have established with Yourgos that I'm here to find Zoubaria, an Early Bronze Age cemetery on Despotiko. He's surprised that I haven't come to see the excavation on Despotiko that the archaeologists have been working on for years. Yourgos Manianos is their boatman. In summer, he ferries the archaeologists and their excavation crews back and forth to the site. But it's winter now, and his boat is moored elsewhere.

On the way across Yourgos reveals that he doesn't know exactly where Zoubaria is. He says it takes all day to walk there and back. My heart sinks, but I'm determined not to lose this one opportunity; if I can't find the graves, at least I can get a feel for the island. I suggest they drop me on Despotiko and come back for me later. We agree on five hours. When we land, the two men lead the way to the excavation site a few hundred metres from shore. It seems I'm expected to at least pay homage.

We walk across freshly planted fields. A new crop of grain is just a couple of inches out of the ground. "Bread," Yourgos says. The fields surround the archaeological site. The ground is tilled right up to the perimeter fence. Yourgos finds a way through the fence and shows me around. There are interpretation panels to explain it all. There's an artist's drawing of what they think one building looked like. From the panels I learn that the site was a Sanctuary of Apollo, dating from the Archaic and Classical Periods. The archaeologists know this from writing on the sherds and stones they've found.

They've been digging here for eight years. Yourgos says there are thirty people excavating sometimes. They have found several large buildings, a marble bathtub, iron tools, even ostrich eggs that suggest trade links to Asia.

But this is not what I came for. After twenty minutes, I tell them I want to get going. They seem dubious about my intentions, but confer for a moment, then point me in the general direction – follow the path towards the first rock peak, but don't go up it. Zoubaria is not there; it's behind that. Go right around the peak, then back further. What's behind the peak, and where to go from there, they don't say. I confirm, with hand gestures, that I must go right around the peak. We confirm again the pick-up time. Then we shake hands, they head back to the boat, and I set off. Walking into this rugged land with only vague directions on a short winter day, I realize my chances of finding a plot of prehistoric graves are slim.

The path is littered with dung. It's sand covered with loose rock rubble, punctuated with frequent upthrusts of different kinds of stone: perhaps quartz, and some kind of dark shale. I move quickly but watch my step: a twisted ankle on this rough ground and I could be out here for a long time waiting to be found. The morning is spectacularly bright, with dew still on the bushes and mist rising off the hills. A light breeze is blowing in my face.

Yourgos warned me there were hunters on the island, going after birds and rabbits. I hear gun shots in various places, including on the right side of the peak. I try to stay in the open as much as possible. When the bushes get thick, I let out a holler to signal I'm approaching. I wish I were wearing bright colours.

The path winds through bushes and stunted cedar. Sometimes the vegetation is over my head. It turns out I can't take a direct line to the north flank of the peak, because a deep gully blocks the way. I'll have to climb part way up the side of the peak, and traverse on higher ground. There are goat paths everywhere. It's not hard going, but there's no single obvious route to follow. I keep working my way uphill and around. I can see now that the island extends into a peninsula to the north. I hear gun shots coming from that direction, so I decide to stay high rather than drop down again once I'm past the gully. I'm halfway up the peak and tempted to go for the top, just for the view, but as I work my way around further I see a second peak, and others beyond that, and I realize I have my job cut out for me.

I wish I had paid more attention to the aerial photos that Yannos Kourayos, the lead archaeologist on the excavation, showed me on his computer in Athens. I wish I had asked him to sketch me a route map to the graves. But I understood that Yourgos knew the way and would guide me. Now I can only try to read the land and imagine my way into the lives of the Early Bronze Age people who lived here. If the graves are on top of a ridge, as I remember Yannos saying, then they might be on the ridge that I can see extending north from the next peak. Between that one and the peak I'm on is another deep gully. There's no way to avoid it, and no visible trail, so I pick a line and begin my descent. The ground is very rough, the bushes hide jutting rocks, and I stumble several times. Once I trip and do a complete summersault downhill before coming to a stop. My hands are scraped but otherwise I'm unhurt.

Shots seem to be coming from below me now, and off to the right, so I holler out my presence again. In a few minutes I'm at the bottom of the gully. I feel invisible and vulnerable down here in the bushes, and immediately start up the other side, aiming straight for the second peak. Near the top I come upon several cavities in the stone. My first thought is rock-cut graves, but I quickly realize they are natural erosions in the stone, hollows just large enough for a goat to curl up in.

I scramble the last few metres to the top. I've been hiking briskly for an hour and I'm drenched in sweat. I pull off my outer shirt, lay it on a bush to dry, and let the sun and breeze dry the T-shirt on my back while I snack on nuts and water. I'm about 150 metres above sea-level. I have an almost-complete 360-degree panorama of sea and neighbouring islands. Only the first peak, behind me, blocks the view back to where I started. The rest of Despotiko is spread out before me, with more peaks and ridges. Off the far end is a smaller, rocky island called Strongili. Geologists believe that Paros, Antiparos, Despotiko, and Strongili were once joined together, long ago. One island, broken in four.

Where to go from here? Time is of the essence; I must quickly narrow my search. I try again to imagine my way into the land. If I'm in the general vicinity of the cemetery, then there are two possible places I can imagine them building a settlement. One is in the lower reaches of the drainage I've just crossed, where it flattens out near the north coast. I can see a small beach down there. If that's where the settlement was, then the cemetery could be on the ridge that curves northward from the peak I'm sitting on. But there's a second possibility, a broad valley opening up like an amphitheatre beyond this peak. It drains gently to the south coast. There's a large sandy beach down there, in a sheltered cove. The valley is enclosed within a long horseshoe ridge that forks off from the northward ridge and leads to more peaks in the distance. The graves could be anywhere along the horseshoe ridge, or on its slopes. It's a lot of ground to cover.

I make a plan: explore the ridge to the north first, and if that turns up nothing then backtrack onto the horseshoe ridge and see how far I can get before I run out of time. I pull on my shirt and set off walking. The northward ridge descends steadily and I realize I'll have to climb back up again if I don't find anything. But I can see a place further on where the ridge flattens out into a little plateau. The ground looks bare there, and disturbed. It's worth checking out.

As I approach the plateau, I hear loud gunshots. There are hunters in the bush not far ahead of me. I think they're on the other side of the clearing. I can hear voices. I see a man's head. I don't know whether they can see me, or how they'll react to me stumbling into their midst. I stop and holler and hold my yellow notebook over my head to show my position. They move off, downslope, and I cautiously approach.

The ground in the clearing has been disturbed. There are a few large flat pieces of rock lying about. But I see no evidence of a cemetery: no hollows in the ground or schists piled together, and no sherds of pottery scattered about. But there's lots of dung. This must be a place where goats congregate. It's sheltered from the wind, on flat ground, with thick bushes nearby to feed on. The plateau goes further. I could keep going, but that's the way the hunters went. Best not to push my luck, or my welcome.

I retrace my steps up the ridge. Rather than go all the way back to the peak again, I decide to take a straight line towards the horseshoe ridge, down through another gully and up the other side. The bushes are thick and high in this drainage, too, and I stumble several times. When I reach the ridge, I find it's flat and wide and the walking is easy. I'm making good time now. I can see a small stone building a few hundred metres away. Approaching it, I come first to a heap of stones and weathered planks. There are some schist slabs mixed in with the rubble. The building is a few steps beyond. It looks like a shepherd's hut. It's on the south-facing slope, overlooking the valley, just below the ridge top, protected from the north wind. The walls are thick and made of stone. The roof is made of wood beams covered in stone slabs, but the roof has collapsed in places. There are four small rooms. In one of the rooms, where the roof is still in place, there's a skeleton of a goat, lying curled on its side. The skeleton is intact, except for a hind leg that's been pulled away. There are ligaments on the bones.

Surrounding the shelter is a perimeter wall. The wall has large schist slabs in it. Inside the enclosure, and all over the ground outside, are pottery sherds. I can see more disturbed ground a short distance away, lower down the slope. I begin exploring, like a dog with its nose to the ground, and suddenly, there they are: graves, hollows in the earth, with schists pushed aside or stacked up nearby. There are bushes and thyme growing all over the cemetery, but there is open, disturbed ground, too, and not one patch of heather, though it's growing everywhere else on the slope. Heather is slow-growing; the other plant species have returned first. I can't see any pattern in the layout of the graves, though some may be hidden, overgrown or silted in. At the lower end of the cemetery there's a large depression in the ground. It looks man-made. There's part of a stone wall half-buried nearby. There's nothing else to see. This is all that remains of a 4,000 year-old cemetery where marble figurines were laid to rest beside human bodies.

I wander back up through the graves to the shepherd's hut and sit on the perimeter wall. The defilement is sobering. There is no joy in this accomplishment, but I feel strangely calm, as if the act of finding my way here has brought me closer to the Early Bronze Age people. The settlement must have lain below me, somewhere in the broad valley that slopes gently down to the beach. The valley is sheltered from the north wind. The slopes are south-facing, with maximum sun exposure for crops. The beach looks like an ideal landing spot. On either end of it are two rocky sentinels that would have made excellent lookouts and defensive positions. One of them reminds me of Kastri, on Syros, with its strata and steep rock face. And here, looking out over this secluded natural paradise, was the resting place for their dead.

Time is running out. I have only a few minutes left to explore. I walk a little further along the ridge and wander down the outside of the horseshoe, towards the north shore. It's a long gentle slope, with much less vegetation. My eyes are drawn to a brilliant slash of white not far below. I walk to it. It's a seam of white, fine-grain marble, breaking through the surface. Farther down I see more white outcrops, all glittering in the sun. Here is a vein of marble rising up out of the earth, bone white, bleached by the sun, slabs waiting to be broken off and carved. The dead coming back, asking to be reborn.

This is the point at which he wishes for a force greater than himself, with the wisdom to see what has to be done. I am not that force. I, too, am uncertain where to go from here. Before things completely fall apart, let us have him contemplate a photograph – any one will do. Let us have him contemplate the surface of the stone.

The surface is pebbled. He thinks of human skin, pebbled, the pucker of an areola. The marble is aged, as skin ages, he thinks, like the faces of those who live at altitude. The face of the figurine is impure, as a young woman's face loses its purity of complexion; the marble is scarred with erosion and discolouration. Things grow on the skin (he has forgotten already the scientific terms). He thinks of lichen, spreading imperceptibly. His attention is drawn to chips, flecks of white. He interprets this rationally, turning again automatically to explanation: these are where metal tools struck, or where stone clinked against stone in the satchel of a looter. He wants to register metaphor instead: this is light emerging, pinpricks in a closed sky, primordial light, traveling all this way to reach us.

He wants to reach through something. To get to something. He feels an opening, a fissure, something calling for tears. He does not know where it comes from.

And then it is gone.

> vagina is entrance to the world
>
> the cave, and the grave, the leaving
>
> > all these entries and leavings –
> > promises of return
>
> death promises return
>
> > first the dying
> > then the long silence
>
> > then the slow division and multiplication into spring

we go with you
always with you

      the force of blows
      the collision of plates –

      each figurine holds memory

      the rains, the bad years

She is at the centre of a great circling.

      the way a shore bird knows the tide
      moss, the oscillations of the sun –

      nature's messages are tactile

          secretions
          salinity
          pressure on a flank

      a grain's rub on a stream-bed stone

He has never been here before. He will never come again. This honor is given only once, and to few. He lays her bones inside the cave, among the bones of the others, and opens the skin they are wrapped in, performing the ritual as he was instructed. The bones around him do not frighten him. They are quiet. His mother's voice has gone quiet, too. She is calm now, the night voyage over, her son's voice saying the words that must be said.

What is given to us is not given to us as a proposition is given to us.

It is given as a new being entering the world.

As a child entering the world is both unique and a renewal of form.

Mountains erode. Wind and water are the agents, sun the energy that propels them. Erosion makes soil, and soil sustains plants and animals.

Dead plants and animals, along with particles of rock and soil, are flushed down rivers to the sea. There they sink and become sediment on the ocean floor.

The sea itself sustains plants and animals. When they die, they, too, become sediment on the ocean floor.

Millions of years pass. Sediment accumulates, layer upon layer. It slowly compacts, millions of years slowly, geologic time slowly, inconceivable time, for us.

The sediment compacts under the weight of more sediment falling on top, plants and animals, crustaceans and sponges, silt and clay and gravel. And under the unrelenting weight of itself, it slowly turns to stone. We call it sedimentary rock.

Limestone is one kind of sedimentary rock. (Shale and sandstone are others.) In limestone you can see the skeletons of plants and animals that once lived and died and sank to the ocean floor. Some of these fossils are 3.6 billion years old. Limestone holds within itself a history of the world.

And limestone in turn changes, through further vast stretches of geologic time. Under its own weight, and through the action of plate tectonics, the sedimentary rock is pressed down deeper and deeper into the earth. And there the heat emanating from radioactivity in the earth's core recrystallizes the limestone, transforming it into marble. Fossils are no longer visible, but the ingredients are still there.

During the metamorphosis from limestone to marble, the stone doesn't melt. It never becomes liquid, like lava. But the newly formed marble is soft, and under the extremes of heat and pressure deep in the earth it can fold and change shape without breaking. With the slow drift of continents and the collision of tectonic plates, this soft marble is pushed up to the surface where it cools and solidifies and becomes new land formations, mountains and ridges. The Cycladic Islands are mountains pushed above the surface of the sea.

This is still going on. Mountains are eroding. Sediment is accumulating on the ocean floor. Sedimentary rock is being formed. Marble is being formed, deep within the earth. It, too, will emerge at the surface one day.[127]

We look at stone and see a lifeless, unchanging mass, the opposite of living things. But perhaps the "primitive" peoples of the world understood the world better than we do when they heard stone speak, when they told stories of living creatures turned to stone.

Each figurine, taken from a vein of marble, holds within itself a memory of the world.

He is full of the analytic spirit, today. Full of the desire to say something with authority.

Meaning, he tries, is something added. Something agreed upon. Or accepted as given to us by the old ones. Meaning is given; meaning can be taken away.

Meaning coalesced around the stone. Story, too. Story was made particular: stone rubbed against stone, dust covered the hands. And the particular was repeated, the form repeated. This was story without end, world without end.

And then the figurine, given into the hands of another, the one charged with the duty of colour, grinding cinnabar and azurite, mixing pigments with resins, dabbing hair, dabbing iris and lips.

The mortal cloaking the undying.

Who owns her – her image, her power?

Who has the right to her? The scholars? The state? The people living on the islands today?

The earth?

Those who knew, are departed.

> Allow the people I encountered during my journey to interview me?

Another day, he adds: The *paint ghosts* may be meaning ghosts, but it is futile to pursue this line of speculation. There is nothing in the archaeological record to help us understand what was painted on the figurines, why it was considered important to paint, say, the hair on the head but not on the genitals. (Were the figurines clothed?)

His mind turns momentarily to a woman he saw in a window.

Something (– someone, I could as easily say) has died.

Their world was full of motion. Nothing was at rest: the sea, the tides, the currents; the wind, the birds and fish. Sun and moon and constellations circled overhead. Everything circled, everything rose and fell. Stillness must have had a particular allure and meaning amidst the ceaseless motions of their world, the ceaseless procession towards death. Death was stillness at the end of it all. It's not hard to imagine them wanting to attain moments of stillness in life. And to be reminded of that transcendent state with an image they could hold in their hand.

Revelation is wordless, propositions a betrayal.[128]

There are libraries of books about how to look at art, but where are the books about touching sculpture? The eye can be directed to see, and what it sees described minutely. But our lexicon of touch is poor. The trajectory of a ball in a socket, the angle of a finger's hinge, the range of motion of a clavicle – these are best described mathematically. There are adjectives for the texture of things, and for weight – but for forms embraced? The contour of border, the cleft of opened space? Imagine – slipping one's arm through the opening of a Moore. Taking the hand of a Burgher of Calais. To go that way into the mind of the artist – and to do so in darkness.

I woke thinking of her again. I think of her constantly. No, not thinking, not even seeing her face anymore. But her presence will not leave me.

We are approaching.

We are always approaching.

Always moving towards our end.

> The protagonist starts writing a story about a love affair – ?

I propose to tell the story of a love affair.

An old couple with folding stools are sitting side by side in front of Manet's *Dans la serre*. They are talking about it – and so unfolds the story of their affair. They were lovers, briefly, long ago. Her man has since died, and though there was once great bitterness in him, for her deception, he has come to accept her offer of friendship. The painting shows a man standing behind a garden bench, talking to a younger woman sitting on the bench. She is emotionally reserved and looking away from him, while he gazes at her with tenderness.

She is wearing a long skirt and a jacket with a hundred little buttons fastened to her high collar.
- Do you see how she is like you were then? On her left hand, even, a ring ...
- We were never married. I was free!
- Ah yes, free to be lonely, like her, untouched, buttoned up, looking away into the distance. She cannot bear to meet his eyes ...
- Because he wants to possess her, he wants to make her his prisoner, just like you! Look at the bars between them, in the backrest of the bench ...
- And look behind him – the foliage of that lush plant – his heart is open to her, but her heart is stone.

Only three anatomical details are incised: the fingers, the toes, and the genitals. (And, sometimes, a line for the spine.) There is no structural reason for them to be incised – the hands and feet could have been made without distinguishing the digits. Or, these details could have been painted on, as were others. But they were incised. This could suggests that fingers, toes, and genitals have a different level of significance.

And think of what is not cut into the stone, but which could have been: anus, navel, nipples, mouth, nostrils, eyes.

But, as always, there are exceptions to confound the generalizations we aspire to: sometimes there are incised lines behind the knees, or lines dividing parts of the body into segments. These are not anatomical details but delineations of territory: neck ends, torso begins; thigh ends, calf begins; calf ends, foot begins. More exceptions appear as I leaf again through illustrated books: figurines without incised genitals; a figurine with wrinkles across her belly; one with arms delineated as incised lines rather than carved in relief. Endless confounding of the desire to say something definitive, to limit her to "this" and "not this" – to make her conform to the needs of our descriptive age. To bring her into history, our history. To be done with her.

Men slip by in the passageway.
My heart leaps up at their song.

Move from grasping at explanation and permanence
towards acceptance of impermanence and mystery – ?

He lifts the capstone off.

He lifts out the bones.

Use Chalandriani as the central and recurring motif – ?

The conflicting signposts, the worthless map, the painted arrows
faded on the stones.

> A circular structure – ?
>
> Begin and end on the Chalandriani plateau,
> where he finds no trace – ?

Something has gone by.

I do not open the museum catalogues any more.

I do not go back to the museums.

        I dream of cottages beside lakes
        and deep cold water.

        I see you running through forests
        your white legs flashing.

        I hear your false words again.

> Do I need to better regulate the verb tenses – ?
>
> Would it help to be more methodical about this – ?

> Should the facts I gathered be assembled in one place – ?

I think of words that would soften her heart.

I shift in my place.

You undo the rope, are already gone.[129]

Late, insomniac, the distance widens.

Her face merges with other faces, once held, once loved.

Too little to hold on to, too much to push out from under.

Sediment turns to stone.

embers riding on furnace-like winds [130]

Breakages – parallels – ?

the figurines	*narrative form*	*what once bound us*
ritually broken	broken	broken

Everything is in pieces.

The hills are burning.

Can there ever be unity again?

Come with me, into story.

        old woman
        sprinkling sweet water on the corpse
        sprinkling pollen, sprinkling thyme –

        BZZZZZZZ
        old man, blind and stooped
        turning this way, turning back
        BZZZZ
        BZZZZZZZ

        children dancing out of reach
        clacking stones in their hands
        CLACK!   CLACK!   (this way!) (over here!)
        CLACK!

        birds wheeling overhead

Her pale skin, her small breasts –

We die, not when our bodies die, but when those who remember us die.

> Add coloured pages to the book – ?
>
> Dun end pages, front and back – the dry earth of the Cyclades – ?
>
> A black page, somewhere inside – ?

write silence –
name the sound that disturbs it [131]

We know what is outside the frame by the shadow it casts.[132]

I keep coming back to this: He is small and alone on the plateau. He is walking across it, aimlessly it seems, though his direction is shaped by the turns of the road and the walls that contain it. I know now what he is thinking – there was a time when you could walk endlessly in any direction.

They knew death would come for them. They knew the necessity of death. The pigments were a dance with death, a ritual sparring. When the figurine was placed in the grave, death was acknowledged the victor.

And the putrefaction of the corpse washed over her.
And the small creatures feasted there.

Rains washed her clean, leaving pale bare death triumphant.[133]

For an instant I hear music. But it stops.

Again the silence.

He looks at words now as objects with which to occupy himself, as things to be moved around outside of himself.

He reads a book and it remains outside.

When he finishes, he begins again.

He thinks: What was once inside is gone. What's left are marks, emptied out, the grey pod of the milkweed after the seeds have blown free.

Sleep eludes him.

He imagines rearranging bones in a grave, making room.

The bones must be cared for, but they, too, are outside.

everything is falling away –
structure is falling away –

the way things fit together, the way things mean

> Print all these structure notes on index cards,
> to be included with the book – ?
>
> Make this part of the book's design – ?
> a pocket on the inside back cover holding the cards, to be inserted in
> the book wherever the reader wants – ?
>
> Or shuffled, ordered, and reordered, at the reader's whim – ?

        they danced the tides
        they danced the currents that filled their nets

Dun ground. Dun dust.

Some conservators use lasers to clean the marble.

        We stand at the beginning of time
              – We stand at the end of time
      All that lies between us
            – Long slow passage of the sea

            Hissing sea

        Time wastes between us

                Rising sea.

[sound: waves on a pebble beach, footsteps approaching and passing]

            She is with us
                  – Always with us
         At first light
                – At last ebb

    It is late
        – The seas are rising
    Others came before us
        – They are gone

            Hissing sea

            There is only sea

                (– and the grave)

                (– never forget us)

                (– the capstone pulled over us)

The villages are abandoned, the olive groves are burning.
The taste of death is in our throats.

The pillars of the temple have split.
The marble steps are blackened, the fields charred.

We stand mute in the square, angry, uncomprehending.
Where is there left to cross to now?

Death is more than one death, or an accumulation of deaths, or an accumulation of sorrows and departures.

Death is one stone.

A woman climbs down into the grave with her dead child. She wants to be buried with her dead child.

Someone climbs down beside her, holds her, says, Listen, what is she saying? She is saying, Let me go now, I want to go now, let me go in peace.

> Take away all references to place – all references even
> to the figurines themselves – move it into the realm of myth – ?
>
> Or, perhaps just the last island I visit slips into the mythical – ?

What is missing in his thoughts are the words that say with precision what it is he does not have.

           seeds passed hand to hand
           pulses, grains

           every opening in the earth
           a reminder –

Where are the words that take us through the surface of things?

                    ... and she pushed me away.[134]

never a clean break with the dead or the living –

we must always let go of something

           birds gather on the cliffs
           the stern rope strains to hold

           waves come ashore empty
           bore holes bring up brackish water

           there is no absolution for our neglect

We have a debt we owe.
We have broken our bond.

The earth is emptied of its store.
We have emptied the earth of its store.

> *I am the woman of the rock.*
> *I am the bones of the land.*

The other species will not mourn us.
They will not mourn our passing.

They will thrive again in our absence.
They will graze in the ruins of our walls.

A stage play – ?

Two pools of light.

In one, a woman, wearing a blank mask.

In the other, a man, sometimes stepping out of his pool to go to the front of the stage and address the audience, then stepping back into his pool to play his role.

Forget? How do you tell yourself to forget?

Every time the neighbour climbs the stairs, I pause.

> (this notch a waist)

I do not ever want to forget –

the way she came to me in the morning

    her hair undone
    telling me her dream

This shall not pass away –

It is not better to forget these things –

    (though she asked me to)

        We are smoke.
        We are ash.
        We are dust.

          (We are smoke.)

        We are silver birch.
        We are bluebells.

Light up over her standing off stage, in the side aisle –

Her lips are moving –

Then light out, snapping to black.

The greater part of a figurine.

The larger part of a figurine.

The upper thighs of a figurine.

[light snaps to black]

> *Cold the night, and long.*
> *We wait by the fire.*
>
> *Long we wait.*
> *Long the night.*
>
> *Our children sleep beside us.*
>
>> *you who sang by our fire*
>> *who danced by our fire*
>> *remember us*
>
>> *(remember us)*

(I try to remember what it is like to sing without ever having seen the words.)

> *Fire cries to us*
> *Feed me!*
> *Do not leave me!*
> *I am cold!*
>
> *We do not feed it.*
> *We do not leave it.*
>
> *We pull our skins closer around us.*
>
>> *sleep silent one*
>> *your work is done*

When there is no sound of her breathing
We lay the skins of her children over her.

Night lays its skin over us.

[lights up]

"She called me from the side of the road.
Her battery was low, her phone was beeping.

I went to her flat.
I couldn't stay.

She said she was fine.
She just needed to rest.

She couldn't stop crying.
I hugged her goodbye.

I was the last person she spoke to."

I'm over the headland now. The wind is driving spindrift of sand across the road. The buildings are shuttered.

I pass a man jogging, in sweats and a wool toque. My rental car kicks up a cloud of dust, but the wind snaps it away. Near the end of the beach, the road forks. The topo map shows straight ahead leads to a dead end. The left fork turns me back inland, and due north. A dog charges out of nowhere, snapping at my wheels.

The road climbs quickly to about 50 metres and levels off. Suddenly, to my left, I have a view over the low plateau I have come looking for. Somewhere out there is Grave 28. I'm carrying the photo in my pocket. There's a flat-topped hill in the middle of the plateau.

The road divides again. The right fork twists up and around onto higher ground, and back towards the coast. I stay left and stop the car and get out, then quickly reach back in for my anorak and hat. There is no one about. Further along the road I see a few houses, but I can see or hear no human activity, only the faint clanking of bells.

I stand there, scanning the plateau, wondering what to do. Somewhere out there, if I've read the books and maps right, is Phyrroges. But where to begin looking for it? The sun is already in the west, and there is a lot of land below to tramp around on. It's dotted with houses and criss-crossed with stone walls. The plateau looks too developed and farmed for there to be any hope of stumbling upon prehistoric graves.

I get back into the car and drive forward slowly in second gear, looking for someone to ask: where is Phyrroges? I pass the cluster of houses, but see no one. The road starts dropping down again, towards the Athalasou valley. That riverbed we walked up is somewhere ahead. The hill with the Louros Athalasou cemetery is coming into view on my right. But the road is deteriorating quickly into deep ruts, and there seems little point in going on. I know what lies ahead; my goal is somewhere behind me.

I return to the same spot. How and where to enter the plateau? I assume most of the buildings below are boarded-up summer accommodations, but still – where to start? My eye is drawn to a compound of new buildings below me. The soil is scoured clean of vegetation inside a perimeter wall. It looks raw and unfinished and I can see no one about, so I decide quickly, put the car in gear, and inch down a rough track towards it.

The track is an open wound across this old agricultural landscape. Chunks of marble have been scraped out and pushed aside by a bulldozer. I drive up to the gate of the compound and turn off the engine. I sit there, feeling more and more dismayed.

The wall around the compound is waist-high, made of marble stones cemented in place. Most of the stones are stained red from the earth, many bear white scrapes and fractures. I can see pieces of fine-grain marble in it. The wall is a slapped-up job, topped with a crudely shaped slab of concrete. At regular intervals along the top are little concrete pedestals holding the ends of thin logs. The effect is American ranch gone Greek. Lying on the top of the wall is blue plastic tubing, carrying electric wires to the perimeter lights and the steel gate in front of me. There are two buildings inside the compound, at some distance from each other. One looks finished. Its walls are pastel pink, the shutters dark stained wood. The other building is still a shell, no doors or windows on it yet. Between them sits a small white chapel with a single bell. Everywhere, inside and outside the wall, lies the detritus of modern construction: pieces of styrofoam, crushed cardboard packaging, empty cigarette packs, plastic coffee cups, empty water bottles, crushed pop cans, wood pallets, lengths of black PVC pipe. In the field next to where I'm parked there are trenches scraped into the earth; it looks like a drainage system. I get out of the car and follow one trench for about 30 metres. Chunks of white, fine-grain marble lie scattered about, and several outcrops of marble poke up through the ground nearby.

I decide to walk to the top of the hill in the middle of the plateau and see what I can see. To get there I first have to skirt the perimeter wall of the compound. As I walk beside the wall, my imagination plays havoc with reason: I keep expecting to see part of a figurine embedded in the wall. I wonder whether the workers in their haste would recognize what they had in their hands.

I reach the end of the compound and discover that the back perimeter wall runs beside an older and higher dry stone wall. The space between them is only just wide enough to walk through. It's full of trash from the building site, but I take this route rather than try to climb the old, shoulder-high wall into another field. Soon the walls diverge: the new wall continues straight. The compound has been plunked down ruthlessly square on the landscape, true to a surveyor's grid but ignoring the topography and the ancient divisions of the land. The old wall sweeps upward in a long curve towards the summit of the hill, separating the tillable fields to my right from rough ground rising on the left.

I follow the old wall. It is a thing of skill and beauty: dry, well-maintained, more than half-a-metre thick in places, with large, lichen-covered boulders in the base. At times it's so high I can't see over it. Suddenly, there are numbers on the wall, spray-painted in red, at intervals. I'm at 19, and soon I come to 20, then 24. What do they mean? Is this land being carved up for building lots? Surveyed for some kind of resort development? I step over the skull of a goat.

I can hear bells clanking somewhere, on the other side of the wall, coming, it seems, from the top of the hill. As the wall takes me higher the clanking gets louder, and now I can hear bleating, too. In a moment low cinder block buildings come into view and I realize there's a farm on the other side of the wall. The wall ends and turns sharp left, beside a track that leads in towards the farm buildings. I am almost at the top of the hill, at the same level as the dirt road I drove in on, on the other side of the plateau. Between me and the road lie fields criss-crossed with stone walls.

Knowing that my only hope of finding Phyrroges is to tap local knowledge, I decide to approach the farm buildings. I turn in on the track, wary of dogs. Quickly I'm on the summit of the hill. I can see more fields sloping away on the other side, and Paros across the sea. I realize that I'm entering an intensively managed farm. First, I pass rows of young grape vines, sheltered from the north wind by a wall: the lower part is an old stone wall, added on top are two layers of cinderblocks, cemented in place. Next comes a fenced field of lush green, obviously irrigated. Foraging in it are goats and sheep, many with babies suckling. They watch me pass. I can hear more and more animals bleating and soon come to an opening in another cinderblock wall, inside of which I see pens full of sheep and goats. I spot a man and a woman working and wave to them. The man returns my wave and, emboldened, I signal that I will follow the track into the main yard to see him. I enter the compound and approach the enclosure where they are working. I hesitate to enter, wondering if I should wait for him to come out to see me. But he gestures and shouts impatiently in Greek for me to come in. I do; he approaches; I greet him in Greek, then point to myself and say "Canada." Then I point to my eye and move my finger away from my face and back and forth around the horizon. I say "Phyrroges" but realize I'm not pronouncing it right. I try the word several times again, varying my pronunciation. The man looks impatient and confused. Suddenly the woman, who has been listening and watching without approaching, shouts out the word. The man comprehends and gestures back towards where I came in. Thinking that's as much as I'm going to get, but sensing more sympathy from the woman, I look over at her. She, too, points back the same way, and says something in Greek. I say thank you in Greek and retrace my steps.

When I get to the gate where I first spotted them, I turn and look back at the woman for help, pointing first one direction, then another, miming which way should I go? She calls out in Greek, but I don't understand. I repeat my wordless appeal. She gestures for me to wait and points to the man, who is following a hose along the ground in my general direction. He stoops and turns on a tap, then walks quickly towards me. I still don't know what's going to happen. He slips through a gate and picks up the hose where it lies in the dirt, dragging it towards the corner of the green field. The hose is gushing water. He puts it into one of two plastic barrels inside the fence, their tops cut down low so the animals can get their heads inside. The animals rush forward. I wonder what to do. Will he point me on my way? Suddenly, he sets off walking briskly back along the track I came in on, gesturing for me to follow. I feel foolish, carrying my notebook, unsure of my footing on the rough ground, beside this purposeful, strong man my own age. He is wearing a wine-red sweater, jeans, and a wool cap, and smoking a cigarette down to the filter. His face is burnt and unshaven, the skin rough and red. He says nothing.

We get to the end of the track, where I first turned in. He stops abruptly and looks out over the fields sloping away in front of us. For the first time he speaks. I recognize only one word, Phyrroges; the rest I understand from his gestures and cadence: this, he is saying, is Phyrroges. He delineates the boundaries – an old stone wall on the far left, the dirt road I drove in on, across from us, and, more vaguely now, it seems, that new compound on the right, or perhaps a little beyond it. I say something in English and he repeats the same explanation, the identical gestures. I nod, and gesture with two hands, opening – an opening in the ground – and say "cemetery?" He shakes his head, once. No. Then, satisfied he has done what the woman urged him to do, he brusquely gestures back to his field, says something which must mean "I've got work to do," turns on his heel and walks quickly away. I call thank you after him, in Greek, but there is no response.

I stand there, looking across the land. So here was the prehistoric burial ground called Phyrroges, and somewhere in these fields was grave 28. I suddenly, inexplicably, find this moving: this is the end of my search, not in some dramatic location, a cliff edge or a mountain top or a remote valley, not with some momentous insight, but here, in farmer's fields, less than a kilometre from the tourist beaches, half an hour's drive from town. That farmer, I realize, is a hill farmer, working intensively the old land, defying the tourism development encroaching all around him. From where I stand, the compound that I parked beside is almost out of sight around the shoulder of the hill. The land in front of me drains to the north, towards the Athalasou river. I can see the upper reaches of the Athalasou valley and the high mountains in the middle of the island.

It dawns on me that I'm looking in the same direction as I did from the Louros Athalasou cemetery. I can't see it from here. It must lie just around the shoulder of that hill farther to the north, closer to the valley. Two prehistoric cemeteries, a kilometre or two apart, on hillsides draining to the same valley and the same river. Somewhere in front of me there must have been an Early Bronze Age settlement, perhaps more than one. And what a prime location: fertile valley bottom land, hillsides for grazing animals, and easy access to a sandy coastline for beaching their ships. Together, these two cemeteries provided burial ground for 700 years. I read somewhere that Louros Athalasou was the older of the two, and smaller. The evidence, scant as it is, suggests that the people stopped using Louros Athalasou after about 300 years, and began burying their dead in Phyrroges.

I start to wander slowly down over the fields, moving left first onto new ground. The light is fading. The sun is dipping towards the hilltop. I come upon a threshing circle. Just like at Louros Athalasou, it's made of schist slabs; here they are turned on their edges and planted upright in the ground. There is an empty glass bottle lying in the middle of the circle. Nearby is an old cedar, a blue plastic shopping bag snagged in its branches. The light is turning golden. A three-quarter moon emerges in the cobalt sky.

Wandering away from the threshing circle, I find several marble outcrops in a corner of a field, and some stone shelters for animals. The old fields, defined by the old stone walls, are large, but in places they are subdivided with fences made of rebar and steel mesh.

More garbage: crushed soft drink cans, beer bottles. Then the bones of an animal.

I wander across the fields, circling back gradually towards the compound and my car. I'm walking beside an old stone wall now, this one fallen down. Someone has thrown a rusty bicycle frame on top. And then, suddenly, there they are again, more red numbers sprayed on the rocks. They're up to 43 now. Number 54 is sprayed on a suitcase-size block of beautiful white, fine-grain marble. The numbers follow me ... 55 ... 58....

I come to a field that has been freshly and diligently ploughed. In another field, the ploughing has just begun: a few rows of thick sod are turned over. I sense someone is trying to reclaim this land, after years of neglect.

A loud snap startles me. It's a plastic shopping bag, snagged on a rusty wire. The wind is picking up.

I turn and leave the track I have been following and make my way directly towards the narrow passageway behind the compound where I parked. I cross a large field, not tilled, covered with stones. The earth is dry and there is little growing, though everywhere there are pellets of hard dung. I keep looking down, hoping foolishly for evidence of the old cemetery – pottery sherds, perhaps, or a fragment of carved marble. There is marble everywhere, in all shapes and sizes, and stained red to varying degrees by the soil, but nothing that my eye picks out as man-shaped.

The sun slips below the hilltop.

I come across another marble outcrop – the fracture lines visible, the thin slabs of fine-grain marble waiting to be pried loose.

I hear shouting, coming not from the farm I have just been to, but carried on the wind from somewhere behind me, in the Athalasou valley perhaps. It sounds like an old woman, calling home her flock, or her man.

My eye is drawn to a heap of large stones in the field. They are recently dug-out boulders. Someone is trying to reclaim this field, too, preparing it for ploughing. If it's the man I met, and I assume it is, I silently salute him: holding on to the land, defying the rising tide of tourist development around him, investing time and hard labour in the future of the farm.

Looking down at the ground as I walk, I realize that I'm looking for some connection to the people who lived here thousands of years ago. Perhaps that has been my unarticulated quest all along. It dawns on me that the one remaining connection is the farm couple I just met, working the same land, grazing the same animals, stepping over the same seams of marble. The connection is the dung of their animals dropped on the fields, and the bones of their animals drying in the sun. That man and woman are not so distant, in their lives and concerns and knowledge of place, from the people who lived here thousands of years ago. As long as they farm, the connection will remain, though the graves of Phyrroges have been emptied and the earth ploughed over for planting.

The distant high mountains are in alpine glow. A white cloud is forming at the summit of Mount Zas.

Rather than go back through the dirty passageway behind the compound, I decide to climb over the old shoulder-high wall I followed in, and circle back to the car on higher ground. The wall doesn't move as I climb up and jump down on the other side. I set off winding my way through brush and rough ground along the slope. The sea is steel blue. The wind has grown harsh and cold. I climb another wall to get back to the car.

Mount Zas is hidden in clouds now. Paros is obscured by dusk and mist. I drive slowly up the track onto the dirt road. I stop and look back over the plateau and the fields of Phyrroges. A single light has come on outside the new compound. There is no light on the hilltop farm. I drive back down to the coast and stop. I walk across the beach and wash my hands in the sea. The sun has set. Mars is rising in the east. I pick up a polished pebble of pure white marble and walk back to the car. There are tire tracks all over the sand.

      Head of a figurine.
      Head and neck of a figurine.
      Head and very small part of the neck of a figurine.

                                The straining at the end to be free.

      Chin and neck of a figurine.
      Part of the neck and torso of a figurine.

                                Remember the land.

      Part of the upper torso of a figurine.
      Torso and legs of a figurine.
      Torso and thighs of a figurine.

                                I remember the land.

      ....

                                Nothing was honest.

      Pubic area and upper thighs of a figurine.

                                Nothing was honest.

      Right thigh of a figurine.

                                Nothing endures.

                                Nothing endures.

Right lower leg of a figurine.
Left lower leg of a figurine.

Lower legs and left foot of a figurine.

Lower legs, feet missing.

If what they teach us is stillness, and nothing more
If they teach us nothing more

If we remember nothing more

    remember

        the texture of stone
        the warmth of stone

        the weight of it in our palm

    remember

        our fingers in loam
        the salt sting of rope

        the wet flood of heat
        when we gutted our prey

Once I was naked against her —

One stone against another stone.

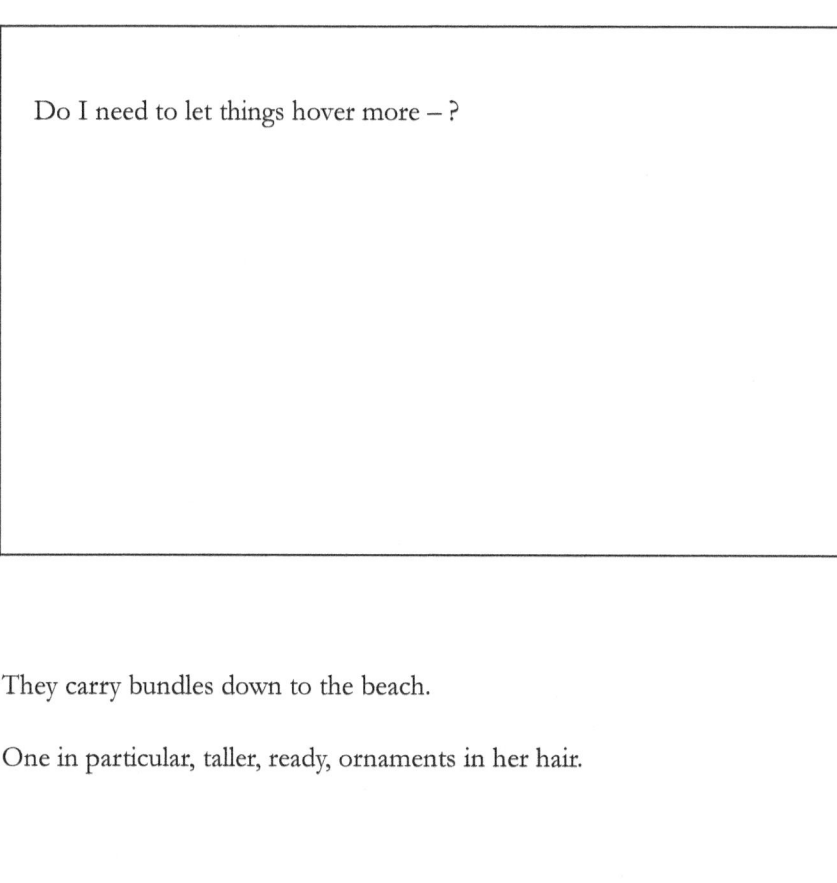

Do I need to let things hover more – ?

They carry bundles down to the beach.

One in particular, taller, ready, ornaments in her hair.

       out of the great pool –
       utterances

       a succession of utterances

            Full knowledge would be death itself. [135]

What do the bones say?

The bones say the time of words is behind us.

The time left to us now is miniscule.

                              Flames illuminate the night.

    Smoke fills the street.

                              Bells clamour in the spire.

....

    Death is a single vaulted cry.

                              Gulls, the perfect sail.

    Children gather in the schoolyard.

                              The doves are silent.

Can it be that all my journeying has been to this end –
to bring goat's milk soap for her fragile skin?

Was the dry white marble preparation for this –
the stillness in the form a rehearsal for her death?

My country is my mother's body.

I have come home to the land of my birth.

[Insert a black page here.]

    Long reach of the oar, winds
    tailed, hissing brine
    the low prow bent for Keros –
    for days we saw no one

>   We rounded point, the north wind
>   catching us, talons
>   falling hard upon us –
>   the meat tough in our mouths with grief

>   ....

I lay under sky and tree. Stones shielded me from the claws of the dogs. Ant found me. Worm found me. It is right the small creatures clean our bones.

>   Lips at her teat, milk on my cheek
>   I was naked against her, long ago

He carried me in his arms. He lay me down gently on my side. He pulled away my skins with decorum. I could do nothing for myself.

>   The dead do not go easily
>   lamentations do not soothe them
>   they stir up trouble in the sea
>   they fear forgetting

I spilt my milk on this land. My breath woke seeds.

>   There is only so much memory
>   one man can hold

>   ....

>   Bones of the dead
>   even these I could not keep from the storm –
>   born dry on board, wrapped in skins

>   she rolled awash in stinging brine
>   knocking fury on the planks of my hull

Not even the scent of my hearth fire left to me.

>   The complaints of the dead are ceaseless
>   they beseech us
>   they assail us with complaint
>   we who must live on

Save me! Why can't you save me?

>   that long night –
>   stars hid
>
>   the dog howled outside the wall
>
>   she howled in my arms
>
>   death tore her flank
>   death dragged her from me

I hear rocks! I hear rocks!

>   O mother
>   could I not have spared you
>   this final terror of the night?

[another black page here]

The lines appear to be parallel, but look closely, the distance between them wavers. They were not made with a single, forked tool. They were made, first one line, then another, freehand in the clay. What is remarkable are the whirlpools these lines swirl down into. There are four whirlpools, joined by the lines, making a four-cornered frame around an image of the sun. The lines sweep over the top and down into the whirlpool. The eye loses them there. You expect something to emerge from the centre of the vortex, but what emerges is on the outside of the whirlpool, another pair of lines under cover of the pair that went in. You trace the lines with your fingers and discover that the two that entered turn back upon themselves at the centre, and rise up out of the whirlpool in the space left between themselves going in. The motion is complex (try it, in the air): clockwise going in and down, which is sun-wise, sinking into the sea; then at the centre, reversing, emerging in the opposite direction, counter to the sun, an upward rush that, once free, sweeps sun-wise again, across to the next whirlpool, and down again. Never ending, never escaping. Always emerging, ever repeating. And look, fish! – swimming in their own orbit, free of the whirlpools, outside the lines. Four fish: swimming hard, swimming free.[136]

I have not written a novel in the usual sense of the word.[137] I don't think that's possible any more. In any case, time is running out.

What I have left is a record of my defeat, a vitrine of broken pieces. And though I am humbled by my failure to make something whole, I cannot help feeling that what I have brought together and put on display is itself an intact image.

When I set off for the Cyclades to see where the figurines came from, I thought I could assemble facts, tell the story of my journey, say something fresh and true. I thought something would speak through me.

This, then, is a record of my defeat. Ideas were plentiful, but unrealized. Some will accuse me of not being equal to the task. But why, when whole figurines stood on display, upright in their glass cases, the masterworks of a culture – why was I drawn again and again to the vitrines where the broken pieces lay?

Impossible to hold all this, in the mind or in the hand. When I look at these pieces now, I see that this could never have been more than a record of things falling apart.

It is hard not to feel that I have failed her.

Where I failed myself was in not being honest.

I have not been honest.

I have not conquered fear.

as death breaks the hold
we break the stone

He sits on a sofa, surrounded by books: books of poems, books of translations, catalogues brought back from the museums. Near at hand are a pot of tea and a cup. It is the one place he feels safe while the enormity of his failure creeps up on him, a little more each day.

There is a woman, too. He watches her writing in the apartment across the courtyard. She smokes while she turns the pages of a book and types, arms stretched out in front of her, the laptop pushed back like an empty plate. She sits at right angles to the window. The sunlight falls across her arm. She lives alone. They went to bed at the same hour last night. When he got up in the morning she was gone.

Observe: The line of shadow moves slowly up the wall.

If she were sitting there now, her face would be in darkness.

Notes

[1] Gennady Aygi, "Continuation of the 'Period of Likenesses'," from *Veronika's Book*, in *Selected Poems: 1954-94*, trans. Peter France (London: Angel Books, 1997), 165.

[2] Ingmar Bergman, preface to his script for *Persona*. My trans. from Bergman, *Cris et chuchotements, suivi de Persona et de Le lien*, trans. Jacques Robnard and Catherine de Seynes (Paris: Gallimard, 1979), 77.

[3] F. N. Pryce and A. H. Smith, *Catalogue of Greek Sculpture in the British Museum*. 3 vols. (London: British Museum, 1892). All figurines mentioned in the Prologue are listed in the museum catalogue, and can be seen online at: britishmuseum.org/research/collection_online/search.aspx

[4] Pryce and Smith, *Catalogue*. Parian means coming from the island of Paros. James Theodore Bent (1852-1897), an English traveller and amateur archaeologist, visited the Cyclades in 1883 and 1884. He opened Early Bronze Age graves in two cemeteries on Antiparos, and donated figurines and other grave goods to the British Museum and a skull to the Royal College of Surgeons, London. See Bent's accounts, "Researches Among The Cyclades," *Journal of Hellenic Studies* 5 (1884), 42-59, and *The Cyclades, or Life Among The Insular Greeks* (1885).

[5] Lesley Fitton, *Cycladic Art* (London: British Museum, 1989).

[6] Percy Clinton Sydney Smythe, 6th Viscount Strangford, (1780-1855) was a collector of Greek and Roman antiquities and British ambassador to Constantinople from 1820-24.

[7] Photograph by John Bigelow Taylor, in Colin Renfrew (author) and Taylor (photographer), *The Cycladic Spirit: Masterpieces from the Nicholas P. Goulandris Collection* (New York: Harry N. Adams, 1991), 106.

[8] John L. Caskey described the plateau: "sloping downward gently, and then abruptly to the sea." Caskey, "Chalandriani in Syros," in *Essays in Memory of Karl Lehmann,* ed. Lucy Freedman Sandler (New York: Institute of Fine Arts, New York University, 1964), 63-69.

[9] See Christos Doumas, "An Historical Survey of Early Cycladic Research" in *Art and Culture of the Cyclades: Handbook of an Ancient Civilization,* ed. Jurgen Thimme and Pat Getz-Preziosi, trans. Getz-Preziosi (Karlsruhe, Germany: Bandisches Landesmuseum 1977), 185-192. Also Christos Doumas, *Silent Witnesses: Early Cycladic Art of the Third Millennium BC* (New York: Alexander S. Onassis Public Benefit Foundation, 2002).

[10] Marisa Marthari, *Syros, Chalandriani, Kastri: From the Investigation and Protection to the Presentation of an Archaeological Site,* trans. Alex Doumas (Athens: Ministry of the Aegean, 21st Ephorate of Antiquities, Ministry of Culture, 1998), 19.

[11] Marthari, *Syros, Chalandriani, Kastri,* 19-20.

[12] Archaeologists call these mysterious clay vessels "frying pans" because they resemble a modern cooking vessel, but there is no evidence that they were ever used for cooking. Some have handles, others have two stubby legs meeting in a V resembling the pubic triangle of the figurines. The interiors of the vessels are hollow and undecorated. The outside back surfaces are decorated with incised and impressed lines, patterns, and images, sometimes highlighted with infilled pigment or a soft white clay called kaolin. The frying pan found at Chalandriani, showing a boat surrounded by interlocking spirals, is pictured in Marthari, *Syros, Chalandriani, Kastri,* 21. There have been rare finds of frying pans made of stone.

[13] Marthari, *Syros, Chalandriani, Kastri,* 26-27.

[14] Interview with Dr. Yannis Maniatis, Research Director, Laboratory of Archaeometry, Institute of Materials Science, National Centre for Scientific Research "Demokritos," Attiki, Athens. 16 October 2005, at his office. Also Y. Maniatis e-mail to me 9 April 2013.

[15] Lila Marangou, ed., *Cycladic Culture: Naxos in the 3rd Millennium BC* (Athens: Nicholas P. Goulandris Foundation – Museum of Cycladic Art, 1990), 152, plate 157. Also pictured in Pat Getz-Preziosi, *Sculptors of the Cyclades: Individual and Tradition in the Third Millennium BC* (Anne Arbor: University of Michigan Press, 1987), 98, 250, plates 31, 32.

[16] Interview with Olga Philaniotou, Director, 21st Ephorate of Prehistoric and Classical Antiquities (now Ephorate of Antiquities of Cyclades), Greek Archaeological Service, Ministry of Culture, 7 November 2005, on board the *Romilda* in the Aegean Sea.

[17] The Museum of Marble Crafts, Pirgos, opened in 2009.

[18] Paul Auster said of his early poems that they "resembled clenched fists." *The Art of Hunger* (New York: Penguin, 1993), 293.

[19] Fitton, *Cycladic Art*, 5.

[20] Interview with J. Lesley Fitton, Curator, Department of Greek and Roman Antiquities, British Museum, London, UK. 28 September 2005, in the museum.

[21] The museum opened in 1986. The Goulandris's private collection has been augmented by donations from other collectors and institutions.

[22] *"Moon of"* : a formulaic phrase from Alexander Marshack's reading of inscribed Paleolithic bone fragments. Marshack, "Upper Paleolithic Notation and Symbol," *Science* 24 (November 1972). Quoted in Jerome Rothenberg, ed., *Technicians of the Sacred: A Range of Poetries From Africa, America, Asia, Europe & Oceania*, 2nd edition (Berkeley: University of California Press, 1985), 582.

[23] James George Frazer, *The Golden Bough*, abridged ed. (New York: Collier, 1922), 591.

[24] For oral testimony about the looting and smuggling of artifacts from Keros during the 1950s and early 1960s, collected from informants on neighbouring islands, see Giorgos Papamichelakis and Colin Renfrew, "Hearsay About the 'Keros Hoard'," *American Journal of Archaeology* 114 (2010), 181-185.

[25] Colin Renfrew, Christos Doumas, Lila Marangou, and Giorgos Gavales, eds., *Keros, Dhaskalio Kavos: The Investigations of 1987-88*. (Cambridge: McDonald Institute For Archaeological Research, University of Cambridge, 2007).

[26] Peggy Sotirakopoulou, *The "Keros Hoard": Myth or Reality?* (Athens: Nicholas P. Goulandris Foundation – Museum of Cycladic Art, 2005), 37. For discussion of Sotirakopoulou's research and book, see the forum in *American Journal of Archaeology* 112 (2008).

[27] Colin Renfrew, e-mail to me, 12 April 2013.

[28] Colin Renfrew, *Cognitive Archaeology from Theory to Practice: The Early Cycladic Sanctuary at Keros*, The Annual Balzan Lecture, vol. 3 (Florence: Leo S. Olschki, 2012), 14. Also: Renfrew, Michael Boyd, and Christopher Bronk Ramsey, "The oldest maritime sanctuary? Dating the sanctuary at Keros and the Cycladic Early Bronze Age," *Antiquity* 86 (2012), 144-160.

[29] See Renfrew, *Cognitive Archaeology from Theory to Practice*. Detailed reports of the 2006-08 excavations, edited by Colin Renfrew, Olga Philaniotou, Neil Brodie, Giorgos Gavalas, and Michael J. Boyd, are published in multiple volumes by the McDonald Institute for Archaeological Research, University of Cambridge, starting in 2013.

[30] *"woman of the rock"* : a formulaic phrase from María Sabina, "The Midnight Velada," trans. Henry Munn and Eloina de Estrada Gonzales, *New Wilderness Letters* 5-6 (1978), 1-4. Excerpted in Rothenberg, ed., *Technicians of the Sacred*, 62-64.

[31] "From 'Battiste Good's Winter Count'," in Garrick Mallery, *Picture-Writing of the American Indians* (Washington: Bureau of American Ethnography, Annual Report No. 10, 1888-1889), 311-314. Excerpted in Rothenberg, ed., *Technicians of the Sacred*, 216.

[32] Stéphane Mallarmé, letter to Henri Cazalis, 30 October 1864. "Paint not the thing itself, but the effect that it produces."

[33] Frazer, *Golden Bough*, 11-14, 32.

[34] Rothenberg, ed., preface to *Technicians of the Sacred*, xxv.

[35] Rothenberg, ed., preface to *Technicians of the Sacred*, xxvii.

[36] Rothenberg, ed., preface to *Technicians of the Sacred*, xxv-xxviii, xxx. See also p. 454: "A typical ritual song practice ... is to repeat (often also to distort) ... one line indefinitely – or as long as the dance & ritual demand – then go on to the second song in the (ritual) sequence, a third, a fourth, etc."

[37] Rothenberg, ed., *Technicians of the Sacred*, 453.

[38] Frazer, *Golden Bough*, 38.

[39] On cultivating sensibility see the remarks by Nadine Gordimer in *The Writer and Human Rights*, ed. Toronto Arts Group for Human Rights (Toronto: Lester & Orpen Dennys, 1983).

[40] Frazer, *Golden Bough*, 45-50.

[41] José Saramago, *Blindness*, trans. Giovani Pontiero (San Diego: Harcourt/ Harvest, 1999), 317.

[42] Michael Ondaatje, *The Conversations: Walter Murch and the Art of Editing Film* (New York: Knopf, 2002), 96.

[43] Stephen Prince, "Throne of Blood: Shakespeare Transposed," essay in The Criterion Collection 2003 DVD edition of *Throne of Blood* by Akira Kurosawa.

[44] Czeslaw Milosz, *The Witness of Poetry* (Cambridge, Mass: Harvard University Press, 1983), 14.

[45] Wisława Szymborska, "Autonomy," quoted in Milosz, *Witness of Poetry*, 45 [trans. unknown].

[46] Simone Weil, *Gravity and Grace*, trans. Emma Crawford and Mario von der Ruhr (New York: Routledge, 2002), 176.

[47] William Carlos Williams, *Spring and All* (1923), reprinted in Williams, *Imaginations* (New York: New Directions, 1971).

[48] Catalogue titles throughout are from Sotirakopoulou, *The "Keros Hoard,"* unless otherwise noted. I have slightly altered some titles.

[49] Catalogue description, Christos G. Doumas, *Early Cycladic Culture: The N.P. Goulandris Collection* (Athens: N.P. Goulandris Collection – Museum of Cycladic Art, 2000), 178.

[50] Patrick Lane, "For Adele Wiseman" in *Last Winter Song* (Madeira Park, BC: Harbour, 2007).

[51] Dylan Thomas, "Do Not Go Gentle Into That Good Night" (1951).

[52] Inspired by "Burial Events" in Rothenberg, ed., *Technicians of the Sacred*, 122, 513. Rothenberg references Rene de Nebesky-Wojkowitz, *Oracles and Demons of Tibet* (1956).

[53] See Czeslaw Milosz, "To Robinson Jeffers" (1963), trans. Milosz and Richard Lourie, in Milosz, *New and Collected Poems: 1931-2001* (New York: HarperCollins/ Ecco, 2003), 252.

[54] Frazer, *Golden Bough*, 357.

⁵⁵ "Ol' Hannah" as performed by Doc Reese, transcribed by Eric Sackheim, *The Blues Line: A Collection of Blues Lyrics* (New York: Grossman, 1969), 26-28. Quoted in Rothenberg, ed., *Technicians of the Sacred*, 76. Reese's performance is on Folkways Records FJ-2801.

⁵⁶ Formulaic preamble to story-telling among the Haya people in Tanzania. Peter Seitel, *See So That We May See: Performances and Interpretations of Traditional Tales from Tanzania* (Indiana University Press, 1980), 107-111. Excerpted in Rothenberg, ed., *Technicians of the Sacred*, 185, 539.

⁵⁷ Inspired by LaMonte Yonge, *Composition 1960 #15*, in Rothenberg, ed., *Technicians of the Sacred*, 514.

⁵⁸ In 1903 Moody formally became headman of the village of Qquuna and was given the Tsimshian name Niiswayxs and the Haida title Nang Gayhildangaay Yuuwans. Robert Bringhurst, *A Story as Sharp as a Knife: The Classical Haida Mythtellers and their World.* (Vancouver: Douglas & McIntyre, 1999), 385, 468 n. 23.

⁵⁹ Robert Bringhurst, *A Story as Sharp as a Knife: The Classical Haida Mythtellers and their World* (1999); *Nine Visits to the Mythworld: Ghandl of the Qayahl Llaanas* (2001); *Being in Being: The Collected Works of Skaay of the Qquuna Qiighawaay* (2001), all published by Douglas & McIntyre, Vancouver.

⁶⁰ Georgia O'Keeffe, quoted in Britta Benke, *O'Keeffe* (Köln: Taschen, 2001), 60.

⁶¹ Bringhurst, *Story as Sharp as a Knife*, 14.

⁶² Bringhurst, *Story as Sharp as a Knife*, 18.

⁶³ Bringhurst, *Story as Sharp as a Knife*, 47.

⁶⁴ Bringhurst, *Story as Sharp as a Knife*, 58.

⁶⁵ Sotirakopoulou, *The "Keros Hoard,"* 29.

⁶⁶ James G. Swan, unpublished diary entry of a visit to the village of Ttanuu, Haida Gwaii, 1883. Quoted in Bringhurst, *Story as Sharp as a Knife*, 101.

⁶⁷ Bringhurst, *Story as Sharp as a Knife*, 115.

⁶⁸ Bringhurst, *Story as Sharp as a Knife*, 147.

⁶⁹ Christos Doumas, "Death" in *Cycladic Culture: Naxos in the 3rd Millennium BC*, ed. Lila Marangou, trans. Alex Doumas (Athens: Nicholas P. Goulandris Foundation-Museum of Cycladic Art, 1990), 95.

[70] Bringhurst, *Story as Sharp as a Knife*, 161.

[71] The sketches are reproduced in *L'Atelier d'Alberto Giacometti: Collection de la Fondation Alberto and Annette Giacometti* (Paris: Fondation Alberto and Annette Giacometti/Centre Pompidou, 2007), 243. The photographs are in *Cahiers d'Art* 10 (1926), 283.

[72] Simon Texier, *Les Architectes de la Memoire* (Paris: Les Éditions du Huitième Jour, 2007).

[73] Bringhurst, *Story as Sharp as a Knife*, 338: "The rest is paraphrase: a fraudulent form of silence." Bringhurst is referring to transcriptions of Blackfoot texts made by Dutch linguists.

[74] Bringhurst, *Story as Sharp as a Knife*, 341-360.

[75] Bringhurst, *Story as Sharp as a Knife*, 382.

[76] Bringhurst, *Story as Sharp as a Knife*, 390.

[77] Olga Philaniotou, 7 November 2005.

[78] Northrop Frye, *The Great Code: The Bible and Literature* (Toronto: Penguin, 2007), 23. Frye calls the three types of verbal expression the hieroglyphic, the hieratic, and the demotic.

[79] Frye, *Great Code*, 25-26.

[80] Interview with Daphne Lalayannis, conservator, Museum of Naxos, November 2005, in the museum.

[81] My variation on lines by Louise Glück: "It is spring! We are/going to die!" from "For Jane Myers" in *The House on Marshland* (New York: Ecco Press, 1975).

[82] Frye, *Great Code*, 28.

[83] Olga Philaniotou, 7 November 2005.

[84] Formerly Pat Getz-Preziosi; she has published under both names.

[85] David Gill, review of *Personal Styles in Early Cycladic Sculpture* by Pat Getz-Gentle, *Bryn Mawr Classical Review* 24 (August 2002).

[86] Sotirakopoulou, *The "Keros Hoard,"* catalogue descriptions for figurines numbered 238, 233, 127, 68, 115, 54, 77, 95, 99, 123, 136.

[87] Frye, *Great Code*, 33-34.

[88] Frye, *Great Code*, 46.

[89] Czeslaw Milosz, "The Separate Notebooks: A Mirrored Gallery (page 24)," trans. Renata Gorczynski and Robert Haas, in Milosz, *New and Collected Poems*, 374.

[90] Bent, "Researches Among The Cyclades."

[91] T. Douglas Price, ed., *Europe's First Farmers* (London: Cambridge University Press, 2000). On lactose tolerance, see Matthias Schultz, "Neolithic Immigration: How Middle Eastern Milk Drinkers Conquered Europe," *Spiegel Online International*, 15 October 2010. http://www.spiegel.de/international/zeitgeist/neolithic-immigration-how-middle-eastern-milk-drinkers-conquered-europe-a-723310.html

[92] Christos Doumas, "The Sea," in *Cycladic Culture*, ed. Lila Marangou, 84.

[93] Ovenden, "The Origin of the Constellations," *The Philosophical Journal*, 3 (1966), 1-18. Cited in Doumas, "The Sea," 84.

[94] Doumas, "The Sea," 84.

[95] Frye, *Great Code*, 85.

[96] Frye, *Great Code*, 71. Hyphenation in the original.

[97] Frye, *Great Code*, 138. Italics in the original.

[98] Carl Sandburg, "Fog" (1916).

[99] Christos Doumas, *Early Cycladic Culture*, 20-39; Christos Doumas, "Cycladic Culture" in *Cycladic Culture*, ed. Lila Marangou, 16-20; Sotirakopoulou, *The "Keros Hoard,"* 47-48, and concordance tables, 342-349.

[100] Milosz, "The Separate Notebooks: A Mirrored Gallery (page 18)," in Milosz, *New and Collected Poems*, 24.

[101] Charles Olsen, "The Song of Ullikummi" in *Archaeologist of Morning* (New York: Grossman, 1973). Excerpted in Rothenberg, ed., *Technicians of the Sacred*, 327.

[102] Stavros Kassandris, conservator, The Museum of Cycladic Art, Athens. Interview 11 October 2005, in the museum.

[103] Willis Barnstone and Tony Barnstone, introduction to Wang Wei, *Laughing Lost in the Mountains: Poems of Wang Wei*, trans. Tony Barnstone, Willis Barnstone, and Xu Haixin (Hanover, New Hampshire: University Press of New England, 1991), xxi.

[104] David Sylvester, *Interviews With Francis Bacon* (New York: Thames and Hudson, 2009).

[105] Exhibition panel, Altes Museum, Berlin, 2009.

[106] Lila Marangou, ed., *Cycladic Culture*. Plates 155, 158, 162; pp. 150, 153, 156.

[107] Rothenberg, ed., preface to *Technicians of the Sacred*, xvii. Rothenberg was referring to "primitive" poetry.

[108] T.S. Eliot, "The Waste Land" (1922).

[109] T.S. Eliot, "East Coker" in *Four Quartets* (1943).

[110] James Joyce, *Finnegans Wake* (1939), 1, line 1.

[111] Olga Philaniotou, 7 November 2005.

[112] Told by shaman Karawe, at Poginden River, Russia, 1896, trans. Barbara Einzig from a Russian version by Waldemar Bogoras. Quoted as "Things Seen By The Shaman Karawe" in Rothenberg, ed., *Technicians of the Sacred*, 302.

[113] Jean Moréas, "Le Symbolisme," *Le Figaro* (Paris), 18 September 1886. Excerpted in Melanie Franke, Silke Krohn, and Dieter Scholz, eds., *The Scharf-Gerstenberg Collection, Berlin*, museum guide, trans. Robert McInnes (Berlin: Prestel Verlag, 2008), 15.

[114] The cemetery in the Grosse Hamburger Strasse is the oldest Jewish graveyard in Berlin, opened in 1672, destroyed by the Nazis in 1943. The nearby Neue Wache building on Unter den Linden, a memorial to the victims of war and totalitarianism, is a room with a hole in the roof, exposing to the elements a bronze sculpture by Käthe Kollwitz of a mother holding her dead son.

[115] Voice of Agnes, the dead sister, in Ingmar Bergman, script for *Cries and Whispers*. My trans. from Bergman, *Cris et chuchotements*, 58.

[116] *The Goulburn Island Cycle, Song 14*, from Ronald Berndt, *Love Songs of Arnhem Land* (Chicago: University of Chicago Press, 1976). Excerpted in Rothenberg, ed., *Technicians of the Sacred*, 397.

[117] Olga Philaniotou, 7 November 2005.

118 The excavation team on Pano Kouphonisi on 7 November 2005 was: Angelos Tsarouhas (Archaeologist), Gabriel Vasilakis (Pick), Fragiskos Anerlavis (Shovel), and Manolis Bardanis (Barrow).

119 Simon Mays, *The Archaeology of Human Bones* (London: Routledge, 1998).

120 Mays, *Archaeology of Human Bones*, 14-15. Other things that may be found by sieving include tapeworm cysts, kidney stones, and calcified blood vessels.

121 Mays, *Archaeology of Human Bones*, 13.

122 Mays, *Archaeology of Human Bones*, 15-21. Also William Bryant Logan, *Dirt: The Ecstatic Skin of Earth* (New York and London: Norton, 1995), 54-58.

123 Tim White, Michael Black, and Pieter Folkens, *Human Osteology*, 3rd ed. (Oxford: Elsevier Academic Press, 2012), 364.

124 Georgia O'Keeffe, quoted in Benke, *O'Keeffe*, 39.

125 Akira Kurosawa, *Something Like An Autobiography*, trans. Audie E. Bock (New York: Vintage, 1983).

126 An afterthought: Why do we assume that all the gods that have ever been are all the gods there will ever be? Perhaps gods are being perpetually born. Perhaps somewhere on the earth, a new god is being born, even now.

127 Sara Eliason, geologist and paleontologist, Curator of Natural History, The Gotland Museum, Visby, Sweden, interview 30 January 2009, Visby. See also: Eliason, *Sunstones and Catskulls: Guide to the Fossils and Geology of Gotland*, trans. Kathy Gow Sjöblom (Visby, Sweden: The County Museum of Gotland, 2000).

128 T. J. Clark, *The Sight of Death: An Experiment in Art Writing* (New Haven and London: Yale University Press, 2006), 105.

129 Wang Wei, "Seeing Zu Off at Qizhou" in *Laughing Lost in the Mountains*, 79.

130 BBC World Service, 8 Feb 2009, 10:00 GMT, from a news report about wildfires in Australia.

131 The evocation of silence, characteristic of Wang Wei's poetry, is discussed in Tony Barnstone and Willis Barnstone, introduction to *Laughing Lost in the Mountains*, xlii-xlvi.

132 Philippe Tauverne, *Le Figaro*, 22 April 1876, my trans. Tauverne was referring to Claude Monet's *L'Été*.

133 See Clark, *Sight of Death*, 235-236.

[134] Ingmar Bergman, speaking of his mother, in *Bergman and Fårö Island*, documentary film by Marie Nyreröd (Svensk Filmindustri and Swedish Television co-production, 2004).

[135] Alberto Giacometti, source unknown.

[136] My description of a clay "frying pan" from Naxos, accession no. 6140 A, National Archaeological Museum, Athens, from a postcard published by the Nicholas P. Goulandris Foundation – Museum of Cycladic Art, Athens.

[137] See Bergman, preface to *Persona*, my trans. from Bergman, *Cris et chuchotements*, 77: "I have not written a film script in the usual sense of the term."

Acknowledgements

I am grateful for the help of many people and organizations during the long gestation of this work.

My thanks first to the archaeologists, for their insights and assistance. In Greece: Yannos Kourayos, Dora Papagelopoulou, Olga Philaniotou, Peggy Sotirakopoulou, Maria D. Tolis, and Angelos Tsarouhas. In the UK: J. Lesley Fitton, Colin Renfrew, and Andrea Vianello. In Canada: Brendan Burke and James Conolly.

Thanks also to Yannis Maniatis, Research Director, Laboratory of Archaeometry, National Centre for Scientific Research "Demokritos," Athens. To Evangelia Kiriatzi, Director, Fitch Laboratory, British School at Athens. To Daphne Lalayannis, conservator, Museum of Naxos. And to Yourgos Marianos, boatman to Despotiko.

Special thanks to Petros Dellatolas, marble worker and artist, Tinos, for his hospitality, generosity, and invaluable insights.

For private study access at the British Museum, London, thanks to Dyfri Williams, then Keeper of Greek and Roman Antiquities, and to J. Lesley Fitton, then Curator, now Keeper.

For private study access at the N. P. Goulandris Foundation – Museum of Cycladic Art, Athens, thanks to Dolly Goulandris, Maria D. Tolis, Peggy Sotirakopoulou, and Stavros Kassandris.

For indispensable assistance in Greece, thanks to The Canadian Institute in Greece (formerly The Canadian Archaeological Institute at Athens), its director, David W. Rupp, and assistant director, Jonathan E. Tomlinson. And to Zoe Delibasis, Cultural Relations and Public Affairs Officer, Canadian Embassy, Athens.

For access to the Library of the British School at Athens, and assistance with research, thanks to librarian Penny Wilson-Zarganis.

For hospitality on Naxos, thanks to Father Manolis Remoundos and the then-resident artists of the former Ursuline monastery in the Kastro, in particular Max Pflugbeil.

Hats off to the excavation crew on Pano Kouphonisi: Frangiskos Anerlavis, Manolis Bardanis, and Gabriel Vasilakis.

The creation of this work was supported by a grant from the Conseil des arts et des lettres du Québec, for which I'm especially grateful. Some of the writing was done during residencies at The International Writers and Translators Centre of Rhodes, Greece; The Baltic Centre for Writers and Translators, in Visby, Sweden; and The International Writers' and Translators' House, in Ventspils, Latvia. Thanks to the directors and staff for their hospitality, to my fellow residents for solidarity, and to the Canada Council for the Arts for travel grants.

Thanks also to Sara Eliason, Curator of Natural History, The Gotland Museum, Visby, Sweden, for insights. To Gary Geddes for critical feedback. To John Bigelow Taylor for permission to use a detail from his photograph of a Cycladic figurine. And to Warren Breckman, Chryssa Charatsi, Dara Culhane, William and Tekla Deverell, Ann Eriksson and Gary Geddes, Christian Försch, Maryke and Paul Gilmore, Bill Harris, Stephen Orlov and Karen Kaderavek, and Heidrun Voigt for helping hands along the way.

None of these people or organizations have endorsed my speculations, and no slight of their work is intended by anything I have written here.

J.G.

www.ingramcontent.com/pod-product-compliance
Lightning Source LLC
Chambersburg PA
CBHW031642170426

43195CB00035B/366